T0368325

Unimaginable

In Your Love is Our Joy

Deacon Francis G. King, Ph.D.

WestBow Press books may be ordered through booksellers or by contacting:

WestBow Press
A Division of Thomas Nelson & Zondervan
1663 Liberty Drive
Bloomington, IN 47403
www.westbowpress.com
844-714-3454

ISBN: 978-1-6642-9793-7 (sc)
ISBN: 978-1-6642-9794-4 (e)

Library of Congress Control Number: 2023907294

Print information available on the last page.

WestBow Press rev. date: 7/17/2023

WESTBOW
P R E S S®
A DIVISION OF THOMAS NELSON
& ZONDERVAN

Table of Contents

Abstract

Human beings want to be happy. We see that in everyday life: from infants beaming with glee to children running around with laughter, from teenagers having fun with their friends to young adults courting their first love with elation, from parents slaving away to make their children happy to grandparents cuddling their grandchildren with delight. Such life experiences led Aristotle, a Greek philosopher from the fourth century BC, to say that the highest good of man is happiness.[1] Henry of Ghent, a thirteenth century Belgian philosopher, pushed the above statement to the extreme by declaring that "a man cannot not will to be happy."[2] I assert that human beings desire more than happiness. They want supreme happiness, i.e., joy. It comes from the fulfillment of our desires. And our deepest desire is to live forever with God.

But we do not need to wait till heaven to receive joy. There is joy here and now. Joy in the will is a choice to do good as a co-creator with God to make the world a better place for one person at a time. Joy comes when we focus on the fruits rather than the pain of our labor. Many people experience joy in their jobs when they bring goodness to others. These jobs tend to satisfy the essential needs of others: physical necessities of food, housing, clothing, medical care, safety, and learning, etc., as well as emotional, mental, and spiritual needs. We receive joy in living when we satisfy our desire for goodness to the best of our abilities. We need to open our minds to know that being a co-creator with God is meaningful, open our will to make the world better place, and open our heart to the law of the gift of self.

The function of the mind is to know the truth. Since Christ is the Truth, joy in the mind is when we are graced with the truth about God: His blessings – to thank Him all the time, His righteousness – to do what is right and good, His love – to reflect it by serving and loving others, His encouragement and perseverance – to do the best we can, His care – to know all is well in His Hands, and His faithfulness – to forever rely on Him and trust Him without hesitation.

Love brings joy to the beloved as the lover fulfills all desires of the beloved by practicing the Law of the Gift of self to the beloved. Love also leads the beloved to become the lover. Both the lover and beloved now experience joy. Joy in the heart is based on the Law of the Gift. Marriage is one of the fullest joys in life. The two lovers become one. Joy in the heart is to become one with our lover. God loves us so much that He wants to be one with us for all eternity in heaven. Joy in the heart is to be one with God and to remain in His love.

God gives us His Kingdom to live in and receive joy. We live in His Kingdom when our mind knows Christ's Truth that God is Good and God is Love, our will does Christ's way of Goodness, and our heart lives Christ's life of love. In God's Kingdom, I rejoice in His Goodness through His numerous blessings in creation, natural or manufactured; I rejoice in His Love through the gift of His all to me as if I am the only person living; and I rejoice in His grace, unmerited divine favor, that He pours into me. I rejoice in the grace of His righteousness, the grace of His faithfulness, and the grace of His Law of the gift.

Jesus wants to restore us to divine health so that we can spend eternity in His Kingdom and thus in His Presence because we desire to be in the presence of the one who loves us more than we can ever imagine. There is no better way to be in His presence than to be one with Him, one with His will, mind, and heart. His will is to save soul; (1 Tim 2:4) His mind is to make us know God (Jer 31: 34), and His heart is to serve. (Mark10:45) Joy is a choice. We pray for the grace to choose to save souls so that by our service, others may know and choose God. Then we live in Christ and He lives in us. (Gal 1:20) Joy comes from being in His presence and love. He is the true source of joy.

God be blessed for His unimaginable love!

Preface

People are preoccupied with the search of happiness. The pursuit of happiness is one of the three unalienable rights guaranteed by the Constitution of the United States. About one out of 3 Americans claim that they are very happy.[3] As happy as they are, they lack joy. Joy, a fruit of the Holy Spirit, (Gal 5:12) seems to be undefinable and illusive. Already, in 1975, Pope Paul VI wrote that the "difficulty in attaining joy seem(s) to us particularly acute today." Almost fifty years later, social conditions have not changed. "Money, comfort, hygiene, and material security are often not lacking; and yet boredom, depression and sadness unhappily remain the lot of many. These feelings sometimes go as far as anguish and despair, which apparent carefreeness, the frenzies of present good fortune and artificial paradises cannot assuage."[4]

In August 2010, just before the third year of my diaconate studies, God gave me at Medjugorje the goal of my ministry. Medjugorje is a little village in Bosnia-Herzegovina about twenty kilometers from Croatia. In 1981, six youths reported the appearance of the Blessed Mother. Although the Vatican has not yet declared the apparition official, Medjugorje has been hosting over a million pilgrims each year. We were there during the Youth Festival. 50,000 people, 35,000 of whom were youth, attended Mass and adoration daily. During adoration, one could hear a pin drop. Throughout the day, 20 to 50 priests speaking different languages heard confessions from people standing in lines that were 15 to 20 people in length. It is a place of grace.

At the top of Apparition Hill in Medjugorje, God blessed me with the gift of divine peace and told me to write about it. Later in the evening, God gave me the goal of my diaconate ministry: to bring peace and joy to all I meet. I had no idea the sources of either peace or joy. But Holy Spirit has not been idle.

At my diaconate ordination in 2012, God blessed me with the grace to draw closer to Christ via the Holy Spirit. He led me to search for ideas, opening my eyes and ears to His messages coming to me through events and conversations with others, and inspiring me to put words on paper. In 2018, I started to work on joy, even though I was editing and rewriting my book on peace. In 2021, I published the book on divine peace, entitled, "Indescribable, in Your Will is our peace." Now, we have "Unimaginable, in Your Love is our joy." Without the Holy Spirit, none of this would be possible. Thank you, God.

Acknowledgement

I praise you, Lord, God Almighty. You are the Light of the World. You come to make our joy complete. You called me to write about joy. You gave me inspirations in a variety of ways. Without your guidance, not a single word would appear. Most of all, you bestowed upon me the grace to listen, to trust and to obey. You also gave me the charisms to write.

Many thanks to my parish, St. Regis, for encouraging me to write. Sincere thanks to the Pastor, Rev. David Buersmeyer for his inspirational homilies, insightful suggestions, and many intangible supports.

I would be remiss not to thank all the professors of Sacred Heart Seminary who taught me about Scripture, Theology, and Pastoral Studies which give rise to the foundational material for this book. I must also thank all the support staff at the Seminary at which I spent almost ten of my most enjoyable years. A word of thanks also goes to all the people who were instruments of God's message to me whether it was from a homily, a casual conversation, a remark, or an experience in life.

I thank my beloved family (children and grandchildren) who not only encourages me to finish the book but left me alone to write. Thank you, Lord, for the blessings of my wife, who made her unconditional, selfless, and limitless acclamation of "yes" to let me complete the work while helping me in numerous ways, like designing the front cover and editing sections of the book.

Whoever reads the words of this book, let him say:
"Thank you God for Your unimaginable Love which
brings us joy."

1. Joy from Free Gifts

On the day I started to write this book at the end of June, my wife was surfing channels on television. The movie, "Christmas Joy," was playing on one of the channels. It was highly unusual to see a Christmas program in June. But it reminded me the expressions of joy on the faces of children when they open their Christmas presents. These gifts are expressions of love for them. There are no strings attached to the gifts. The beloved gives them unconditionally and generously. Expression of love in the form of such a gift is clearly a source of joy to the receiver. And they include gifts of food, charitable deeds, kindness, help, and prayer.

Gifts to fulfill one's desire

Joy in eating ice cream

The joy of receiving gifts that are free, unconditional, and selfless.

One of the favorite things that a grandfather does is to give ice cream to his grandchildren, especially when they have never tasted it. They express the joy of eating ice cream with beaming smiles and glowing eyes. I also love to give them chocolates for the first time. Spoiling is unconditional. It is usually selfless unless one points to the joy that grandparents partake in the joy of their grandchildren. At that age, the grandchildren may not understand love or selflessness. But they sense that it is an unconditional action. Such action brings them joy. The taste of ice cream and chocolates also helps to enhance their joy.

In spoiling the grandchildren, I must be cognizant of their desires. My youngest granddaughter likes sour stuff, e.g., lemons or grapefruits, while her older sister likes sweet stuff. So, I only give sour stuff to the youngest one, while sweets to the older. Fulfilling one's desire is a primary source of joy. And the greater the desire, the more is the joy. For example, there is more joy in consuming food when one is hungry.

One time, as I was leaving a hamburger joint, I saw a person standing at the door begging for money. I invited him to come into the hamburger store to choose what he wanted and paid for the food. He was totally surprised by what I did. He did not expect the gift of food, nor be treated with dignity to choose what he wanted to eat. He was happy and appreciative. Joy comes from fulfillment of his desire for food and respect. What is our deepest desire? Does Christ satisfy it? "To a hungry man, Christ is very lovely when He has a loaf of bread in His hand."[5]

For what do we hunger? We, human beings, having the construct of body and soul, wants to live. Food, therefore, is a great desire. But our deepest desire is to live forever even though Satan tries to convince us that it is not possible. And God, in His great love for us, satisfies our desire by giving His Only Son so that whoever believes in Him may have eternal life" (John 3:16) with Him in heaven. There is no greater joy or quality of life than living a life in the presence of someone who loves us. Many psalms from the Old Testament describe the joy of being in the presence of God. (Psa 95:1-2, 16:8-11, 32:11, 67:2-5, 96:11-13) Satan tells his favorite lie that no one can live forever because of cellular aging.[6] He uses the fear of death to curtail our activities. Today, some people are still unwilling to eat at a restaurant because of fear of the Covid-19 virus.

Paul said that he longed to depart this life and be with Christ, which is better than to live. But he also said that life is Christ. (Phil 1:21-26) Indeed, joy of life whether on Earth or in Heaven comes from being in and with Christ. Here we sense the continuation of joy from earth into heaven and its permanency.

In the above example, the man will be hungry again in six to eight hours. His joy was short-lived. To make his joy enduring, we must fulfill his desire of independent survival, i.e., appropriate, and lasting employment.

Four years after the 1967 racial riots in Detroit, Father William T. Cunningham and Ms. Eleanor M. Josaitis established Focus Hope of Detroit to bridge racial division and bring hope back to the city. Focus Hope started by providing food for pregnant and post-partum mothers, infants, children prior to school age, and seniors.[7] Now it has programs on early learning, job training, and youth development. Its volunteers provide free of charge

Joy comes from fulfillment of desires

Jesus showing fish and bread credit: motortion, from istock / Getty images plus

What is our deepest desire? Does Christ satisfy it?

training in life-long skills in technical areas, leadership, behaviors, personal interaction, and work habit. Securing a job for a graduate is part of the job-training program. Focus Hope does not just give the hungry a fish. It teaches them how to fish, fulfilling their deeper desire to be independent and self-sustaining.

Most of us, however, are not called to be like Fr. Cunningham or Ms. Josaitis. But God does call us to help others whenever we can. Help satisfies the desire of another, thereby bringing joy. Often, we are called to help within our profession, which is normal as we all strive to achieve a common goal through teamwork. Helping outside our daily job requires compassion and mercy. An ophthalmologist, son of a parishioner, spends his vacation in Africa to provide medical help free of charge. We can also help outside of our expertise. My pastor spent his vacation in Texas at a border town to help immigrants from Mexico before the Covid Pandemic of 2020.

> ## The Name of Jesus
>
> *When we ask in Jesus' Name, we shall receive, and our joy will be complete. (Jn 16:24)*
>
> *What do we ask? Do we ask Him to be His instruments to save souls?*

There are many diverse types of help. For example, some parishioners volunteer to drive people to Mass, bring Holy Communion to the homebound, cook and deliver a meal to the sick, or provide emotional and spiritual support to those having challenges in life. During Covid Pandemic, volunteers made phone calls to the elderly or brought groceries to others. These are some corporal works of mercy which Jesus outlined in His Judgement of Nations (Matt 25: 31-46)

Many issues may prevent us from doing corporal works of mercy. But there are always spiritual works of mercy, which include giving instruction, advice, console, and comfort to those in need. Forgiving and bearing wrongs patiently are also spiritual works.[8] Prayer, especially praying for others, called intercessory prayers is a major spiritual work of mercy. Here we must let God help us with our prayers. He knows what everyone needs, including those for whom we are praying.

We, as beloved children of God, share in the anointing of the Spirit. Through Him, we have the authority to minister others in the name of Jesus. And when we ask in His name we shall receive, so that our joy may be complete. (John 16:24) That is why we sing praises to His Name. (Psa 92:2) Prayer unleashes, not only the power of healing, but also the unlimited divine power for us to continue the salvific mission of Christ. It removes any obstacles that may hinder His plan for us as His instruments in saving souls.

God fulfills our desires

God fulfills our desires with numerous gifts as seen in the box on the right so that we can be joyful. Most obvious are the gifts of the planet Earth and the wonders of life sustaining processes, e.g., the Oxygen[9] and the Geobiochemical[10] Cycles. The Sun and the Moon, of course, play an important part in the above cycles. Elements in these cycles work together meticulously. God did not leave anything to chance. The cycles critically provide the much-needed oxygen, carbon, nitrogen, water, phosphorus, iron, and other minerals needed to support the great gifts of life and freedom to human beings. Life and freedom are addressed in later chapters.

Our Heavenly Father knows that we need food, drink, and clothing (Matt 6:32) and He provides them to us together with shelter, job, friends, and relatives. Every day, we use many things to make our lives easier and more convenient. We

---

Some unconditional gifts from God

- *The universe with all its wonders: sun, stars, Earth, flowers, lakes, mountains, animals, plants, and natural processes to sustain life,*
- *Our life, freedom, talents, inborn personalities, educational and career opportunities,*
- *Family, spouse, children, parents, friends, and colleagues,*
- *Food, shelter, clothing, flushing toilet, running water, hot water boiler, furnace, and fridge,*
- *Transportation and communication technologies,*
- *Music, art, video games, exercise equipment,*
- *Television, microwave ovens, computers, I-pads, and cell phones,*
- *Medicines, and medical equipment,*
- *People with talents to invent the above.*

Hence," rejoice always and give thanks to God in every circumstance." (1 Thes 5:18)

---

take them for granted. Two out of ten people in the world have no electricity in 2012;[11] 60% of the world population have no flushing toilets in 2013;[12] 780 million of them having no safe drinking water in 2020.[13] In the United States, we are blessed with these things and other conveniences like hot water showers, microwave ovens, and cell phones. We cannot live without computers or the internet. Again, God be blessed for the city planners who put in all over the country sewage lines, water pipes, electric transformers, cell phone towers, etc. Let us also thank God for inventors of furnaces, air condition systems, stoves, ovens, refrigerators, etc. Can you imagine how unhealthy we would be without all the inventions in the medical field, from medicines and supplements to medical equipment, like MRI machines, and so forth? They are all gifts from God. We cannot spend enough time thanking God in our everyday life for all His blessings

One of the ways to thank God is to enjoy His gifts. Take time to eat and enjoy our food, even if the chef is no good. Spend another 15 seconds under the hot water in the shower, especially on frigid winter mornings. Following Paul, we must rejoice always and give thanks to God in every circumstance. (1 Thes 5:18) We rejoice in God's gifts, which are unconditional, selfless, and limitless. Blessed Solanus Casey even teaches us to gives thanks to God ahead of time.[14]

Vacationing on a camel

We cannot spend enough time thanking God for all the good things in life.

One of the ways to thank Him is take time to enjoy His gifts.

When I was working, I used to think that my successes were due to my ability to learn and work hard on the job, and my associations within the company. God was out of sight and out of mind. But then I realize, God created me with inborn personality and talents. God gave me the opportunity to pursue an education which taught me to think and search for knowledge. God blessed me with jobs and bosses who allowed me the freedom to be creative. Literally, God even arranged my marriage. I thank God especially for my children. God blesses my children with good health, appropriate skills, and intellect. They have grown up to be responsible contributing people to society. They have their own families. They are graced with faith in God and many of His gifts. When good things happen to us, they happen not out of luck or accident. They are results of divine providence. If we just spend some time to write down God's blessings to us in the past week, we will realize how much He loves and blesses us.

What we tend to miss are the enjoyments. They may include taking a walk by the lake watching ducks and swans amidst the setting sun, strolling through a botanical park smelling the roses, vacationing on a camel's back, window shopping at a mall, serenading in Vivaldi's Four Seasons being played by the virtuoso Cho-Liang Lin, immersing in Monet's Water Lilies in Giverny amidst shadowing clouds and sunlit reflections in the water, calming an infant in a mechanical swinging and bouncing chair with nature sounds and music, playing video games, persevering on an exercise machine, or simply watching a program on a large flat screen television. Everything is a result of God's blessings to make the world a better place: from creation to creative knowledge and from inborn talents to inspirational inventions.

Grace is the unmerited divine favor given to us by God. All that we have comes from His grace. It is not a surprise that God gives us so many gifts because Jesus tells us that if we who are wicked know how to give good gifts to our children, how much more will the Heavenly Father give good things to us if we ask Him. (Matt 7:11) But we get all these things when we often do not ask. Jesus also says, "seek first the kingdom [of God] and his righteousness, and all these things will be given you." (Matt 6:33) Hence, we take God's grace for granted. Of course, there are also people who can amass wealth unscrupulously.

Do we return God's grace with gifts and blessings of our own onto others? The Consecration of bread into the Body of Christ reminds us how Christ offers Himself for the salvations of souls. In fact, the words of Consecration are: "this is my body which will be given up for you." God gives Himself to us to fulfill our desire for eternal life in heaven. As members of the Body of Christ, i.e., His Church, do we give up our body for another to make the world a better place? Do we try to do good for others and thereby fulfill their desires and give them joy?

"This is my body which will be given up for you"

The Sacrament of the Last Supper, 1955 by Salvador Dalí; © 2023 Salvador Dalí, Fundació Gala-Salvador Dalí, Artists Rights Society

Do we give our body to make the world a better place for another, thereby, fulfilling their desire and give them joy?

2. Joy in the Will

Because joy comes from the fulfillment of our desires, we must have the freedom to do what we desire. Next to life and dignity, the freedom of choice is God's greatest gift to us. He gives us this gift at the beginning of creation. Although God commanded Adam and Eve not to eat of the fruit of the Tree of the Knowledge of Good and Evil, (Gen 2:17) He did not prevent them from disobeying the commandment. There was no fence around the tree, nor did God made the tree so tall that they could not reach the fruit. Alas, they listened to the serpent and ate of the fruit. Likewise, although God gave the Ten Commandments to Moses and the Israelites, (Exod 20:2-17, Deut 5:6-21) He never insisted that they or we obey them. David, the greatest Israeli king, chosen by God, committed murder and adultery. (2 Sam 11)

> *Freedom to satisfy our desires gives us joy*
> ――――――――
> *Freedom is the greatest gift from God next to life and dignity.*
> ――――――――
> *Therefore, it is a source of joy. But it is not joy. It could be a chain on joy.*

Chains on Joy – Disobedience

Surprisingly, though freedom is a source of joy, it can also be a chain on joy. Are we tired of people telling us what to do? Is this why we dislike our bosses? We call two-year-old children the Terrible Two's because the only word in their vocabulary is "No." From an early age, we suffer from the mindset that disobedience is freedom.

Do we recall that regardless of the risk, we would drive before we are old enough to get a license, snuck in the first alcoholic drink, smoke the first cigarette, or even ingest the first marijuana? Our parents told us that we needed to avoid all those things. Yet we wanted to do these forbidden things.

The game of bogeyman was a favorite past time with my grandchildren. I would be the bogeyman and chase them around the house. The chasing gave them the license to run, scream, and yell around the house, all of which the parents would not allow. They had a lot of fun. They beamed with joy. I do not remember playing bogeyman with them outside the house.

In the above examples, the joy comes from the desire to do something forbidden and so we rebel against laws and rules. Paul said that the Mosaic Law, which encompasses moral, legal, and ritual rules, is holy (Rom 7:12) but apart from it, sin is dead. (Rom 7:8) He is telling us that though the Law is good, it also provided opportunities for the Israelites to say "No." In fact, the original sin committed by Adam and Eve was their disobedience to the decree not to eat the forbidden fruit. We see that disobedience can have severe consequences. Criminals, who desire to disobey the law, when caught, are put in jail. They and people who live under a dictatorial government desire freedom to do what they want. Today, there are also criminals who put others physically in chains in the form of forced labor and sex-trafficking.[15]

This desire to disobey is evil per Augustine. He confessed that while he was a teenager, he stole pears, not to eat but to throw them to the pigs. Although Augustine condemned his action as foul, he loved it. He said that "I loved my error--not that for which I erred but the error itself … seeking nothing from the shameful deed but shame itself."[16] Augustine was not on a guilt trip or wallowing in shame. He used this experience to kindle in him a sense of "Divine Un-Ease that drives him close to the Lord."[17] In other words, Augustine, recognizing that disobedience is wicked, advises us that we should use the fleeting joy of disobedience to get closer to God, the source of all joy.

Disobedience is a desire of freedom and a chain

Credit LeManna, from istock / Getty Images Plus

Augustine says the joy from it, if any, should drive us closer to God.

Chains of unfulfilled happiness – the Past

Many people are not happy with their past. My friend, Rob, lamented, when I visited his beautiful house on a lake, that he just missed purchasing a better house on the other side of the lake two years ago. Rob let the past dampened the joy of his present situation. A more serious example on the chains of the past is separation. Children with a past of rejection, unhappy childhood, stringent parents, an overburdened lifestyle, or family conflicts may strive to escape their past by moving away and live in another state resulting in a separation with families.

Our past: possessions, careers, or addictions which may give us riches, fame, pleasure, or power can be a chain on our joy when we are not satisfied with them. They may include food, money, art, boats, cars, alcohol, drugs, political or corporate ladders, video games, the internet, or work. A Chinese parishioner loves to cook. Joy in cooking is consummated when others enjoy the food. Those who ate her food acclaim her as a great cook. In her younger days, she would throw big parties. She would cook multiple dishes of food over a period of 2 weeks. Because people enjoyed her cooking, she would hold these parties every year. They became a tradition and became a chain on her as she grew older with changing interests.

> ## *Past chains on freedom*
> ―――――――――――
> *They come in the form of possessions, careers, or addictions to riches, fame, pleasure, or power.*
> ―――――――――――
> *Lack of freedom is lack of joy. Are we chained by past unfulfilled happiness?*

We know that we cannot serve both God and Mammon (Matt 6:24) and that the latter alone does not make us happy.[18] We do well to listen to Jeremiah: "Thus says the LORD: Let not the wise boast of his wisdom, nor the strong boast of his strength, nor the rich man boast of his riches; But rather, let those who boast, boast of this, that in their prudence they know me." (Jer 9:22-23) We should be chained to the knowledge of God.

An overburdened lifestyle from the past may be a deterrent to joy, e.g., damaged family history over generations could be a chain on happiness. Indigenous groups in Canada,[19] Native and African Americans in the United States,[20] Black people and people of color in South Africa,[21] or single parents in the United Kingdom,[22] are the poorest in those countries. Generational poverty can lead to a destructive/dysfunctional lifestyle. For example, alcoholism is a common issue among Native Americans because they used it to cope with the loss and the stress of colonization. It then became an element to define one's individual and tribal identity. Later, it became a protest against both the Indian and the White cultures.[23] Such a history severely impacts adolescent Native Americans in their choice of an identity and a life, curtailing joy.

They need to focus on the present as we hear, "Thus says the Lord, … remember not the events of the past, the things of long ago consider not." (Isa 43:18). Human beings are created very good. (Gen 1:31) Hence, we cannot be bad regardless of our past. Besides no amount of regret can ever change the past. Paul understood this when he told the Ephesians not to lose heart over his imprisonment for them. (Eph 3:13, Acts 21:27-37) Indeed God will make all things work for the good, especially for those who love Him. (Rom 8:28) Also, the present, i.e., the life in the present, is a gift of God and so are all the blessings of the day. When we focus on the grace that He gives us today, it will get us through today and every day. God is in control, and He will help us every day, "See, I am doing something new! Now it springs forth, do you not perceive it? In the wilderness I make a way, in the wasteland, rivers." (Isa 43:19)

Chains of unfulfilled happiness – the present

A common chain on joy in the present is the feeling of loss. It could be a loss of health, home, job, possessions, future opportunities, and/or love. They can be caused by abnormal events, e.g., birth defects, accidents, pandemics, wars, natural disasters, abuse, and/or crime. Loss can also be come from normal life experiences like growing old, corporate buyouts, economic downturns, or breakup in relationships due to divorce and/or death. Losses are usually real. But they can also be imaginary. For example, an inferior complex could lead to the feeling that my parents love my sibling more than me resulting in an imaginary loss of love. Overcoming such imaginary losses may require mental help.

Ken, a parishioner, suffered the evil of cerebral palsy. The damage to his brain was so severe that he spends his life in a wheelchair with no muscle control to his legs and his right arm. His right arm is tied down to his wheelchair to avoid spastic motion. He can barely move his left arm and fingers.

> *Life in the present is a gift from God*
>
> ---
>
> *and so are all the blessings of the day.*
>
> ---
>
> *So, dwell not on the past but rejoice in God's gift of the present moment.*

The first emotional response to loss is fear of not knowing how to cope with the loss. For example, if I were Ken, I would fear about living since I cannot feed myself, dress in the morning, take a shower, and so on. Fear arises when we do not know who we are, what we can do, and/or how God helps us. Fear fills our mind with darkness drawing it away from God.

Then the loss may overwhelm and over-stress us. For Ken, even though he learnt to be patient and not be frustrated by all the things that he cannot do or took a longer time to do, he is bothered, not by his own physical inabilities, but by the impatience of adults taking care of him. Doubt creeps in as to whether he can find someone who can really help him. When we doubt that no one, especially God, loves us enough to help us, sadness and anger set in. Doubt puts a limit on our heart in perceiving God's love causing us not to trust in His guidance, protection, and grace. When our heart fails to recognize God's love, we are far from Him.

Then the loss may lead to desperate greed in trying to replace the loss, e.g., Ken may resort to robbery to get enough funds to find good help. Finally, hopelessness takes root in us when we realize that there is no way to replenish the loss, especially the loss of love. Joy comes from the love of God. When Satan successfully drives us away from God in mind, heart, and will, he has succeeded in taking away our joy.

We suffer from an absence of joy when we live a life of fear, doubt, and greed, which Satan uses to tempt us in time of loss. Rather than focusing on being a co-creator of God in making the world a better place, life becomes a means to satisfy our covetous will, to yield our heart to the doubt that we are not loved, and to fill our mind with the darkness of fear.

Overwhelmed with loss

Credit: JaaackWorks from Getty Images Plus / istock

Satan uses fear, doubt, and greed to tempt us in time of loss to drive us away from God.

To handle any sort of loss is not to dwell on it. Acceptance of the loss allows one to move on to search for another worthwhile purpose. Ken practices what Paul encouraged the Corinthians: "We are afflicted in every way, but not constrained; perplexed, but not driven to despair; persecuted, but not abandoned; struck down, but not destroyed." (2 Cor 4:8-9) God blesses Ken with the grace to accept things as they are and not to dwell on them. He is not chained to his present condition. Rather, he focuses on the good things in life: the people who help him, nonstop learning and teaching, and how he can contribute to society and God. Lately, he has been trying to convert his Protestant friends to become Catholic.

Paul was in prison when he wrote his letter to the Philippians. Although it was a letter of exhortation on unity, the words of joy and rejoice appear at least fifteen times. He was telling them to be joyful and rejoice with him and in the Lord. He was joyful because, even arrested, he was able to accomplish his life's purpose of preaching the gospel, even to the whole Praetorium (Phil 1:13) and Caesar's household. (Phil 4:22) In the face of all his difficulties, Paul said: "In every circumstance and in all things, I have learned the secret ... I have the strength for everything through him who empowers me." The secret for Paul is trusting and finding strength in Christ. He is the author of good things in life and help us to fulfill God's purpose in life. (Phil 4:12-13)

Sometimes our jobs feel like a prison, eight hours a day and five days a week of doing the same thing. Often, we ask: "What profit have we from all the toil which we toil at under the sun?" (Eccl 1:3) In the parable of Prodigal Son, (Luke 11:15-32) the older son refused to join the party given to celebrate the return of his younger brother after spending his inheritance. The older son was over-burdened, tired of working, and felt bound to the job and the father. He had no contentment though he was providing food for others. Instead of recognizing that he was bringing joy to others, he viewed himself as a slave. He had lost hope for a better future like the two disciples on the Road to Emmaus. (Luke 24:13-35) Without hope there is no joy. Hope is found only in God. We cannot base our hope on our bosses who are more interested in their careers. Hope on political leaders to fix our society is futile since they are interested just in getting re-elected. Even hope in our friends may sometimes not come true because they are too busy with their own lives.

Cerebral Palsy

Credit: ferrantraige/ Getty Images E+

Secret of accepting things as they are is trusting and finding strength in Christ to fulfill God's purpose. (Phil 4:12-13)

When we just focus on the labor of our jobs there is no hope. We must focus on the fruits of our labor. Since almost all jobs, as shown in a later chapter, are essential for the survival of human beings, what better fruits can these jobs produce. An analogy to the pains of labor is the pain that a mother feels at the time of giving birth. She, however, forgets the pain, though it remains, when the joy of seeing her baby overwhelms it. In life, the fruits of our labor will make us forget its pain. We must always choose to focus on the fruits of our worthwhile purpose to serve God and others, and not on the labor. Paul, when facing death, focused on the fruits of his work which resulted in sacrificial service of the Philippians. (Phil 2:17) But we realize that sometimes we may never see the fruits of our labor. When we do our best in serving God, He will make sure that our work will wear bear good fruit. We note that neither the one who plants, nor waters are anything, only God causes the growth. (1 Cor 3:7)

But we must also recognize that we cannot answer the call to discipleship in a lukewarm manner. In the Parable of the Returning King (Luke 19:12-27) each servant received a gold coin to engage in trade. The king entrusted those who earned a profit with the responsibilities to govern cities. He also gave the gold coin of the wicked servant who did not earn any profit to the one who had made a profit of ten gold coins. "To everyone who has, more will be given, but from the one who has not, even what he has will be taken away." (Luke 19:26, see also Luke 8:18, Matt 8:12, 25:29, Mark 4:25) As disciples, we must be conscientious and persistent as stewards of God's grace (Eph 3:2) to serve Him as "slaves of the Lord Christ." (Col 3:24, Rom 1:1, Gal 1:10) When we do so, God will give us more grace to serve Him. On the other hand, if we decline to accept and make use of the grace, we lose it. In Matthew's Parable of the Talents, the master threw the wicked servant "into the darkness outside, where there will be wailing and grinding of teeth." (Matt 25:14-30)

Focus on fruits not labor

Blog: "Still Life, Life Stilled." Courtesy of the National Gallery of Art, Washington D.C.

Be conscientious slaves of Christ and stewards of His grace even if fruits may not be known.

Chains of unfulfilled happiness – the Future

The future in the most simplistic term is what one expects the present would become. Lofty expectations for me, my colleagues, subordinates, or others are chains on joy because when unfulfilled, they cause severe disappointments. One of the pastoral associates at my parish has the expectation that everything must be done according to her way. She spent hours writing down detailed instructions for volunteers who serve as sacristans, environmental coordinators, Eucharistic ministers, etc. Then she complained that no one did things her way and that she had to spend time working late into the evening straightening things out. There is no joy in one's life when one insists on "my way or the highway."

Other expectations may include the desire for a better job, another promotion, improved health, bigger house, more money, faster car, obedient children, or more lovable spouse. We strive to belong or strain to do one better to satisfy our ego. Expectations, in reality, are things that we think will satisfy our ego. Although we tell ourselves that we must crucify rather than satisfy our ego, we still spend most of our time wanting more or better of what we already have. But nothing will ever satisfy this inner "want" because it is really our ego. The end result is that we become a lover of worldly things. And the "lover of the world is an enemy of God." (Jas 4:4)

One of the ways to satisfy our ego is to do something new or challenging. People talk about their first-time adventures in bungy cord jumping or diving off a cliff. Aside from providing the excitement of not knowing what to expect, e.g., the adrenaline rush of free falling, they challenge us to overcome fear, a huge satisfaction for our ego.

Another ego satisfier is control. My wife's older brother, in his youth, would ride his bicycle, not holding onto the handlebars but holding onto the hands of his cousins also on bicycles. The three of them having linked together via outstretched arms would be riding their bicycles abreast about ten feet across. They would have taken up the whole lane of traffic. Of course, they had to overcome the challenge of riding at high speeds trying to keep up with the speed of automobiles. They were joyful, not just because they overcome the challenge, but they were violating the law while controlling the traffic. Here we have a triple sense of joy: disobedience, power to control traffic, and overcoming a challenge. Of course, police arrested all three youths and summoned their parents to the police station.

Crucify rather than satisfy our ego

Christ Crucified, 18th century German sculptor, from Pepita Milmore Memorial Fund. Courtesy of the National Gallery of Art, Washington D.C.

We want more and be in control of all things, even our joy.

Instinctively, we want to be in control. It makes us independent, which is a pre-requisite to survival. My oldest grandson gets his kicks from verbally picking on his own siblings. He would rile his younger brother on his dietary choices, his lack of skills in schoolwork, playing sports, or video games, or just about anything. He gets his joy by seeing his younger brother react in an angry manner leading to perhaps a fight which the older boy would always win. He also knows that his parents forbid him to gain the upper hand or play tricks on his siblings as a result of his superiority. But disobedience and showing off his dominance mean that he is also in control. He gets triple joy in doing what he does. Being in control means power, and power corrupts. Hence, my oldest grandson continues to pick on his younger brother.

> **Joy is fruit of the Holy Spirit**
>
> ---
>
> **Only God can give us joy.**
>
> ---
>
> **Joy comes from being in the presence of Christ**

We even try to control our joy. We try to drown out our sorrow, frustration, disappointment, or anger by drinking alcohol, taking drugs, or having some obsessions. We may also try to find things that will give us more pleasure like going on vacation, parachuting out of an airplane, or acquiring more possessions, like clothing, art pieces, televisions, or even pianos. We hunger for Fridays so that we can do something different on the weekend, but then Monday comes again. These secular things may temporarily cause us not to remember our pain. At the end of the Last Supper, Jesus told His disciples that they will weep and mourn when He dies on the cross. But their anguish and pain will be lifted when they see Him again. (John 16:20-22) Our joy comes from being in the presence of Christ. It will cause us not to remember our pain or sorrow. Only God can give us joy. After all joy is the fruit of the Holy Spirit. (Gal 5:22)

Freedom to make the world a better place

In the previous sections, we discussed the misuse of freedom to disobey, dwell on glory or ills of the past, focus on labor rather than fruits of our work, and fulfill our ego. Instead, we need to use our freedom to do good because God ingrained us with His Goodness when He created us in His image and likeness (Gen 1:27). Goodness is His Being, His essence, because "No one is good but God alone." (Mark 10:18) Hence, we desire goodness and is inclined to do good. Following Plato, we can exclaim that "good has rightly been declared to be that at which all things aim."[24] This desire and inclination for what is right or wrong are written into our hearts[25] as Ezekiel proclaimed: "I will give you a new heart, and a new spirit I will put within you ... so that you walk in my statutes, observe my ordinances, and keep them." (Ezek 36:26-27).

Indeed, Cain knew, long before the commandment that "you shall not kill," (Exod 20:13) that murdering Abel was wrong when he said that his punishment was too great to bear. (Gen 4:13) In contrast to the negative precepts of the Ten Commandments, the Sermon on the Mount provides positive teachings on observing God's statutes.

Jesus teaches that we need to "seek first the kingdom of God and his righteousness." (Matt 6:33) The kingdom of God is the reign of God. Seeking His reign is to obey Him. Righteousness is what is right and just in the eyes of God. Since none of us is just (Rom 3:10) or righteous, we rely on God to discipline us (Heb 12:6) in our way of life, just like I would not let my grandchildren play with fire.

> ### Seek first the Kingdom of God and His Righteousness (Matt 6:33)
>
> ---
>
> *Seeking His Kingdom = obey Him*
> *Seeking His Righteousness = to do good*
>
> ---
>
> **Let us make doing good into a devotion: doing it with care, diligence, promptness, and frequency as His co-creators in making the world a better place for someone.**

By His grace, He channels our desires to please Him, (1 Thes 4:1) i.e., to do what is good, since He is Goodness itself. To please someone, we must know him/her. Hence, we must be chained to the knowledge of God. "No one knows what pertains to God except the Spirit of God." (1 Cor 3:11) So, let us always ask for the Holy Spirit, (Luke 11:13) which already resides in us through our Baptism. (Acts 2:38)

God in His immense love for us has equipped us with all that we need to make seeking His righteousness the purpose of our life. What better righteousness is there than to make the world a better place for one person at a time. In His great love for us, God has also given us His gift for excellence, which enables our will to make things better. But we must choose to exercise the freedom for excellence unless we have the personality of a super achiever, like my granddaughter, who wants to be and is usually number one in all she does in academics, music, sports, etc. This gift of freedom for excellence "not only makes us do good but also do it carefully, diligently, and promptly."[26] I would also add "frequently." Then we have made doing good a devotion. Yes, God calls us to devote ourselves to be a co-creator with Him. He, who loves us more than we can ever imagine, has created this beautiful planet Earth, some of the beauty of which is shown in the figure on the previous page. And He gives us dominion over all this beauty, charging us to make His good creations even better. Hence, our worthwhile purpose in life is to make the world a better place for one person at a time.

Joy in the will comes from being a co-creator with God.

HIGHWAY 401, ONTARIO, CANADA

BOYNE MOUNTAIN RESORT, BOYNE, MI

PAINT POT YELLOWSTONE PARK, MT

CHAPEL ROCK MUNISING, MI

God's creation is good and beautiful. Can we make it better?

We, who are very good, can make what is good even better. When we do so, we satisfy our desire for goodness and get joy.

Paul used God's co-workers (1 Cor 3:9), co-workers in Christ Jesus, (Rom 16:3) or co-workers for the kingdom of God (Col 3:11) to address those who ministered to bring others into the faith. Indeed, as co-creators with God, our purpose is to make others know and choose God through our work of making the world a better place for them. It is through this work that we make known of God's love in creation. And through our actions of goodness in serving others, we make known His continuous love for them. He blesses us with His grace to realize these two purposes. When we choose to live them and to live them with excellence, we satisfy our desire for goodness and we receive joy in the will.

> **Joy in the will is a choice to do good to**
>
> - be a co-creator with God,
> - make the world a better place for one person at a time,
> - make others know and choose God by our work, and
> - do it with excellence.
>
> Such a choice affirms God's love in creation and His continuous love for us.

3. Joy in Living

Life is a joy because it is God's greatest gift. He gives us life because He loves us. Over 10% of the population in the reproductive age in the United States was infertile in 1997[27] and infertility affects as many as 1 in 6 couples[28]. Two of the three children of a friend married husbands who are barren. Sadly, even couples who can produce children may outlive their children. Another friend, Steve, was filled with joy when his daughter-in-law gave birth to her first child. The joy was short lived because the grandson turned out to be severely handicapped. At the age of four, he still had to rely on a feeding tube and a respiratory aid. He died shortly afterwards. Steve was ecstatic when his second grandson was born in perfect health. Sadly, he died of crib death a year later. Now Steve has adopted grandchildren.

Because life is a gift from God, it itself is joy. Infants who are loved and felt that they are part of the family, waddle in happiness when their physiological, safety, and relational needs are satisfied as formulated by Maslow.[29] They smile innocently and beam with joy.

"Life is a joy."

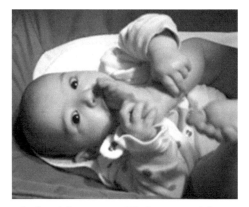

Infant beams with innocent joy.

Because it is God's greatest gift.

The joy of creating life

Women are blessed. They carry life within them when they become pregnant. The joy of pregnancy is often characterized as exuberant, lively, and effervescent. One can literally see the joy in their faces. Their hair becomes finer and brighter and their skin, smoother and shinier, thanks to an increase in blood supply. Their breasts and curves also increase in volume. They have higher vitality due to better eating and healthier habits. The love for the baby, most likely, drives these habits. One can see the joy in mother's eyes and the smile on her face as she caresses her tummy, feels the kicking and movement of the baby, and/or tells of her pregnancy even though she is enduring nausea, discomfort, restless sleep, and/or other medical conditions. And this love for her baby can be so pure that the mother will carry the baby in her heart for the rest of her life regardless of how long he/she lives. I surmise that a mother will love a child for 100 years even though he/she may live only 90 years.

Amidst severe pain of contraction and delivery, she receives the ultimate joy of giving life. (John 16:21) The joy of giving birth is impossible to describe in words. Some mothers try to describe it as an ecstasy, the excitement of crossing the finish line, the delight of looking at the face of new life, the elation of holding the newborn infant in their arms, and/or the thrill of knowing that life has been created through them. The joy of childbirth must be experienced.

50 years ago, fathers were invited to witness and even be part of the birthing process. The wonder and joy on their faces at the time of birth tell of the joy in giving life. They were part of the conception process, and now they will enjoy nurturing life. There will be countless hours of joy in hugging and holding the infant baby regardless of all the challenges of feeding, cleaning, and/or clothing him/her. The father, for the first time, throughout the pregnancy, experiences this joy of creating new life when he takes hold of the baby and relishes in his/her liveliness. He anticipates and takes joy in all the work associated with raising the child. The joy of parenthood is evidenced by the love of unconditional gift of self.

> ### *"Joy of parenthood"*
>
> *starts with conception, through carrying the baby in the womb and giving birth, to watching the child growing into adulthood and senior status.*
>
> *Joy of parenthood is evidenced by the unconditional gift of self. Parents worry about their children beyond their death.*

God commanded Adam and Eve, and hence all humanity, to be fertile and multiply. (Gen 1:28) Doing what commands is joyful. (John 15:10-11) Satan wants to take away this unique joy of giving life. Many societies in this world, falling for his pervading lie that we are free to decide whether our babies live or die, have adopted pro-abortion laws. All people who support abortion are complicit in the crime of murder. An article from the National Institute of Health says: "embryonic and fetal life are a continuum, within which are time sequences and points."[30] This life evolves from conception to cellular development, and eventually to a fetus with heart, mind, will, and limbs. And this life will continue to evolve from infancy to childhood, and from adulthood to senior status.

Joy in saving and protecting lives

The instinct to protect and save lives comes from God's essence of goodness. My oldest grandson and second oldest granddaughter at the ages of five and six, respectively, would hold on to their sisters who are two years younger, especially in a crowded area or crossing the street. My son, at the age of five, did the same thing with her younger sister when we attended a function at the Detroit Art Institute. At that age, in a crowded environment, the taller adults would overshadow them and prevent them from seeing their parents even though they might only be three or four feet away. The expression on the younger child changed immediately from a feeling of apprehension and fear to that of assurance and placidness because of the protection offered by the older sibling. There was a smile on the face of the younger child, a sense of quiet joy. At the ages of 5 and 6, the protective reaction of the older sibling was by instinct and not by reasoning.

Joy in being protected and saved

Younger sister is in the protected presence of the older one.

The instinct and opportunities to protect and save come from God's goodness.

This same instinct would lead us to save and protect lives when God gives us the opportunity to do so. My father-in-law, during the Sino-Japanese War, carried a sick child on his back and walked over twenty miles to find a doctor. The roads were war-torn by constant spraying of bullets and bombardment from Japanese aircrafts. A trip that would normally take less than an hour by car turned into one that took three days on foot. There was no food or water except what one could carry. My father-in-law was willing to die to save the child's life. When he brought the child home, healed and safe from the Japanese aircrafts, the parents were filled with joy because a new life was granted. The family is so grateful that the children of the child would still show their appreciation to us whenever we visit them in Hong Kong by feeding us immensely at the best restaurants.

The medical profession is a noble one. During the coronavirus pandemic, between March 2020 and April 2021, 3,607 of these professionals lost their lives to save lives.[31] We, who are the recipients of the gifts of physical salvation from the medical profession, have experienced great joy from their services. Workers in the field of physical health are broad and numerous. Just to name some, they are doctors, dentist, aids, nurses, first responders, hospital workers, audiologists, pharmacologists, eye glass and hearing aid providers, nutritionists, gymnasium owners, exercise trainers, etc.

We must also thank all support personnel for these professions. They would include, for example, management, investors, accountants, sales and marketing personnel, administrative assistants, equipment designers, manufacturers, repair persons, inventory and delivery people, janitorial staff, and all others who are part of each of the above operations. In the rest of the chapter, I shall continue to list professions and their support personnel which are essential to supporting life.

The prime example of dying for the good is the willingness of soldiers, firefighters, and police personnel to die to protect lives. We recall the heroes of New York City when they charged up the Twin Towers of the World Trade Center on September 11, 2011. They offered their lives for the love of others. Jesus teaches us that there is no greater love than laying down one's life for one's friends. (John 15:13)

> *"Saving and protecting lives"*
>
> *bring great joy to the recipients.*
>
> *Many professions are involved in saving and protecting lives: e.g., medical, first responder, health care, police, fire, hospital, product designer for their safe usage, etc.*

There are other professions involved in saving lives. As an example, my brother worked in the field of automotive safety for over 50 years. His research was instrumental in developing seat belts, front air bags, side intrusion beams, air bags on the door, and headrest. In 2013, there were 32,000 deaths due to car accidents. Seat belts alone saved over 12,500 lives.[32] Here we can include people who design and/or engineer products for safe usage, like cars, microwave ovens, or airplanes. Let us thank them and their support personnel.

Ingrained with God's image (Gen 1:27) and, therefore, His Goodness, we desire goodness. When created to work together to make the world a better place for one person at a time, we fulfill our desire to do good, and hence, are joyful. We are more joyful if our good efforts are successful, but their success depends on God.

Joy in nurturing lives

Parents are important co-creators with God, not just in reproducing lives or providing basic needs to their children, but in teaching them how to live. They teach them how to be human, in particular, how to exercise the three faculties of the soul: the will to do good, the mind to know the truth, and the heart to love. And the quickest way to learn is through examples. The parents must live lives of goodness, truth, and love. Sadly, few children thank their parents while they are alive for their teaching and sacrifices, but in their heart, they rejoice in being a human adult. We include all who nurture others, e.g., coaches, mentors, pastors, those who run day care centers, etc.

Teachers have a tremendous responsibility to nurture their students. There can be no greater joy or tribute for a teacher than a student telling him/her years later how much they have relied on what they had learned in making a life for themselves. A parishioner sent me this story. A math teacher asked her students to write something nice about each of their classmates. She collected the papers and wrote, for each student, a list of nice things that their classmates said about him/her. One of the students, Mark, joined the military and was killed in action some years later. At the funeral one of his fellow soldiers came up to the math teacher and asked if she was the teacher that Mark always talked about. After the funeral, the father of Mark showed her what they found on Mark when he died --- the two pages of good things that the other students had said about him. Many of Mark's classmates have also kept those pages within reach in their lives. In her own way, this math teacher has taught the students how to live a life of goodness by noticing their own goodness through the eyes of others. With God, she created a life of goodness one student at a time.

> ## To be co-creators with God, we can
>
> - *save, protect, nurture lives,*
> - *make lives safer, and*
> - *provide basic needs physically, emotionally, mentally, and spiritually.*
>
> *We are joyful as co-creators with God because we make lives better for one person at a time.*

Teachers, like parents, bring up one child at a time as a beloved child of God, beaming with His Goodness and Love. Most important, they teach the children how to learn, values to keep, and truths to believe in. In nourishing their children, they make lives better for them, bringing them joy in their lives. Teaching is, therefore, a noble profession. Not only, are they essential workers, they are often tasked to give themselves totally, including their lives, to teach children the truth that they are beloved children of God. Again, we must include all support personnel for the teachers.

Both parents and teachers can rejoice in their challenging work and sacrifice when their children grow up with the understanding of giving themselves for the good of others. Like Christ, they are called to serve and not to be served. (Matt 20:28, Mark 10:45)

Joy in providing basic needs

Providing basic needs to improve the health of others is an important way of making lives better for them. Food, clothing, shelter, safety, and sanitation are just some of the elements that are necessary for physical health. They serve to illustrate that many jobs are essential.

Can you imagine what it would be like if we have to grow our own food, raise our own chickens or cattle, and fetch our own water? What inconveniences did we suffer during the supply chain shortage of 2022? Many people in numerous professions are involved in getting food to a grocery store, e.g., farmers, ranchers, food preparers, cleaning and packaging people, shipping and transportation workers, receiving and stocking employee, cashiers, etc. All these people are called essential workers in the coronavirus pandemic of 2020. Let us not forget all their support personnel.

As wealthy as we are in the United States, basic needs are not always available for everybody. Over half a million people are homeless[33] and thirty-seven million people are hungry, one in seven households.[34] God be blessed for all who provide food to them.

Everyone who work to bring food to others need to recognize the joy that they bring with the food. But alas, how many people thank them for what they do? We are so set and so content with our way of life that we forget the joy of convenience and be grateful of it. Gratefulness consummates joy.

Clothing and shelter are the next two basic needs. We can create similar lists of personnel involved in getting clothes to a department store or building material items to a hardware store and thank them for what they do to make our lives better.

Empty shelves

We take for granted the convenience of grocery stores.

What are the different jobs that bring food, clothing, hardware, etc., to a store? What does it take to run a school, hospital, or car plant?

In almost all homes, we have safe drinkable running water, electricity, flushing toilets, and heat. Let us, therefore, be grateful also to our city planners, builders, workers, plumbers, electricians, producers and salespeople of equipment, energy, and water, etc., and support personnel, who provided such conveniences to us. Let us also be grateful to all who keep our cities and homes clean.

Providing basic needs

brings joy to their recipients. At the same time, it should give joy to those doing it for they are making the world a better place.

Are we grateful to those who provide basic needs for physical, mental, emotional, and spiritual health? Do we thank God for His Hand in this work?

Health includes emotional, psychological, and spiritual needs. Emotionally, those who bring pleasure to the senses, for example, beauty to the eyes, scrumptious taste to the palate, fragrant aroma to the nose, pleasuring sounds to the ears, or velvety texture to the touch, bring joy to others. We also need to be legally and financially healthy. Communication and transportation workers provide the means for others to freely talk when they wish and go where they want, thus bringing freedom and joy. Aside from mail carriers, phone, internet, broadcast, and parcel service personnel, we must include those who help others with relational and interpersonal skills. Relaxation and entertainment are crucial to emotional health. Excitement is another driver of emotions. Sporting events and adventures in life bring excitement. They bring joy to those participating and those just watching the events.

The main aspect of psychological health is mental. There is a wide range of mental disorders. They vary from severe mental deficiencies to minor degeneration in memory due to age. Numerous professionals, e.g., psychologist, psychiatrists, neuroscientists, etc., provide services to improve mental health.

In this world of brokenness, many look to God for help in dysfunctional families, marriage difficulties, loss of a loved one, severe sickness, and so on. Sadly, the number of pastors and priests are declining even though they will tell you the joy they have had in their lives. My pastor in his 42 years as a priest finds joy in serving his parishioners and seeking their wisdom. The work of pastors and parishioners is collaborative. Numerous lay ministers and volunteers work together to make a parish thrive and grow.

Happiness

I listed numerous vocations to show that almost every worker and job are essential! And there are many other vocations which I had not listed but should include. We work together as co-creators with God to make lives better and more joyful. In this way, we focus our lives towards doing good for others. Deep contentment comes from knowing we are doing good and bringing joy to another person.

Happiness is defined as living a good life with a sense of meaning and deep contentment.[35] Bringing joy to another is meaningful. It is also a life of deep contentment because joy is contagious. We are joyful when another is joyful. Let us look at what it means to live a good life. Life is good when we are successful in what we do. Per Pascal,[36] we can measure success by our accumulation of riches, power, fame, etc. As discussed earlier, the problem with this measure is that we become

> **Bringing joy to others is happiness.**
>
> **Happiness = good life with meaning and deep contentment**
>
> Good life is not success in accumulation of riches, fame, power, or in using our talents but in being kind and generous
>
> Good life with meaning = make the world a better place
>
> Dignity of work = contentment
>
> **Almost everyone works to make the world a better and more joyful place.**

chained to these material things. How well we use our talents is another measure of success. The problem with this measure is that we cannot choose to ignore our talent. Being good at logic and processes, I would arrive at a solution to a problem before my wife does, to her chagrin. With her perfect pitch, she would be annoyed when someone goes out of tune in a musical performance. Our talents have become our chains.

How kind and generous (holiness to Pascal) we are when doing good for another is the third measure of success. Do we spend time helping others, listening to their problems, or saying a kind word to a stranger? The amazing thing about this measure of success is that when God gives us the opportunities to help others, we have a choice to be kind and good. It is a choice that surpasses this life since Jesus is the ultimate model for this measure, and we want to be successful in the eyes of God. Furthermore, this type of success does not oblige us to renounce success in the other two measures. A good life is, therefore, defined by how kind and generous we are when doing good for another.

Pope Leo XIII defined labor as exertion of "oneself for the sake of procuring what is necessary for the various purposes of life, and chief of all for self-preservation."[37] There is no better purpose than to make the world a better place and at the same time procure wages for sustenance of one's life. That is the dignity of work or labor. But between 2020 and 2022, we have severely diminished the incentive to work, devalued the dignity of work, and taken away the joy of the fruits of labor because the United States Government provided $931 billion stimulus payments to about 165 million individuals during the Covid-19 pandemic[38] with child tax credit, food stamps, etc. Since welfare paid better than the median income for millions of Americans, less than 40% of the new jobs created in September 2021 were filled.[39]

We also note that work is work with others.[40] In this modern world, although the principal resource is man himself, it is his disciplined work in collaboration with others[41] that can transform the world. The new adage is that Rome was not built by one person alone. We must have working communities.

The law of the gift

We are joyful when we devote our lives to worthwhile purposes as co-creators with God. Devotion means doing the best we can. We note that God created us with the purpose to be His co-creators. He equipped us with talents and His charisms. He gave us help to choose an identity and a vocation even though many things in life seem to happen by chance. All good things come from God. He then gives us the opportunity to make sacrifices to achieve the purpose of our lives.

The law of the gift

The gift of a dandelion flower shows that giving is ingrained in us.

It is in giving joy to others that we receive joy. Let us go and bring joy to others!

Contentment comes from sacrifices. We saw in the last chapter that when we view the job as a routine, we just work. We must focus on the fruits of our labor and the sacrifice to achieve their purpose. Often, God calls us to do extra service and make additional sacrifices. The bigger the sacrifice, the bigger the contentment. At one time, three parishioners, who were lawyers, provided pro-bono legal services to others. One of them helped wrongly accused inmates to petition for their release. When I asked him why he was doing such work, his answer was, "if not me, then who?" They brought joy to their "clients." It is this joy that makes us give of ourselves to help others to make the world a better place for them.

The gift of self is called the law of the gift. It is ingrained in us. My oldest grandson was slow in learning how to walk. He was over two years old before I took him out for his first walk in the park. Everything fascinated him. He saw dandelion flowers for the first time. The bright yellow flowers stood out in a sea of green grass. He stopped at the first flower and looked at it intently, studying it, touching it, and admiring it. He asked if he could take it with him to give it to his mother. So, I helped him to break off the flower. He held it tenderly all the way home. At that early age, he had not yet learned the art of giving. So, he threw it at his mother, thereby bringing her immense joy. He instinctively knew that giving something pretty and different is an expression of love which he needs to return.[42]

> Joy in living is to satisfy our desire for goodness to the best of our abilities.
>
> - Our mind knows that being a co-creator with God is meaningful.
> - Our will desires to make the world a better place for one person at a time.
> - Our heart wants to practice the law of the gift of self.
>
> When we open our mind, will, and heart to God's grace, we receive opportunities to do good, giving us a joyful adventurous life.

From the beginning of the bible to its end, this law of the gift, the gift of self, forms the heart of Christian teaching. Abraham gave his only son, Isaac, as a sacrifice to God. (Gen 22:1-18) Jesus teaches that "whoever finds his life will lose it and whoever loses his life for my (Christ's) sake will find it." (Matt 10:39, 16:25) And Jesus loses His life for our sake.

When we satisfy our desire for goodness, we receive joy. Joy comes from bringing joy to another. Like my father-in-law and the math teacher, God gives us the opportunities and the adventures in life to give of ourselves to make the world a better place for others. Hence, joy in living is to open our minds that being God's co-creators makes life meaningful regardless of our sacrifices, our will to make the world a better place, and our hearts, to the law of the gift of self.

4. Truth and joy in the mind

Joy in the will comes from satisfying the desire of doing something good, the best that we can, while joy in living, from opening our mind, will, and heart in the giving of self to make the world a better place for one person at a time. The will acts when it is supported by rationale in the mind. The mind must be convinced that making the world a better place is good. It must also know who we are and what we can we do.

> *Human beings seek truth, but what is the truth?*
>
> ---
>
> *Was it true that George Washington cut down a cherry tree?*
>
> ---
>
> *Truth is not popular opinion. It corresponds to objective reality.*

The function of the mind is to seek the truth. John Paul II defines a human being as "the one who seeks the truth."[43] Augustine said that "none ... wanted to be deceived."[44] Hence, the truth is what every human being seeks. Aristotle says we are the "only creature ... who knows that he knows, and is, therefore, interested in the real truth."[45] When we know the truth, our mind is joyful.

What is truth?

Truth is not popular opinion. For example, most people say that George Washington cut down a cherry tree when he was a young boy and admitted the truth to his father showing that he was an upright man from boyhood. Is it a true story? This story has never been verified and may never be verified. In fact, it may even be false.[46] Sadly, today, we are brain-washed to take popular opinion as the truth. "Opinion is power ... and dominant ... What is shown and 'appears' (on television, for example) is stronger than reality ... is becoming more and more the real governance of the world."[47]

Truth is defined as a fact or something that corresponds to objective reality, which means what is real at a point in time. For example, the yearly death rate in the United States from the flu virus is now over 500,000 rather than about 36,000 because of COVID-19.[48] This truth is based on empirical fact. In the age of empiricism,[49] only empirical data were viewed as truth. Rationalism burst onto the scene in the 17th century when Descartes, a French philosopher and mathematician, uttered the famous words: "I think therefore I am,"[50] and continues today. Hence, our mind arrives at the truth when reasoning corresponds to objective reality, i.e., what is real at a point in time. For example, the objective reality in 2022 that the coronavirus is more contagious but less potent can lead to the reasoning that the virus will be around for a long time, but we need not fear its deadly effect. Such a reasoning can be called a truth.

But reasoning alone fails to explain all truths like miracles which happen every day. In particular, miracles of uncorrupted bodies[51] or healing[52] are hard to explain. Because we are still in the age of rationalism, people try to explain everything through science. Stephen Hawking, a theoretical physicist and cosmologist, said that the universe cannot be explained by a finite set of statements.[53] He was citing Gödel's Incompleteness Theorem. It states that if a system is defined by a set of axioms in the system, it is incomplete. In other words, if all the laws of physics are packed into one theory, it would be incomplete. Reason and faith are required to determine the truth.[54]

Revolting against rationalism, philosophers in the 19th and 20th centuries focused on the individual and his/her choice of freedom. They ushered in existentialism at the cost of obliterating emotions and relationships with phrases like "hell is other people"[55] and "God is dead."[56] This centering on "I" has moved us into always asking the question, "What's in it for me?" This question has caused many news reporters to air opinions rather than facts resulting in the proliferation of "fake news" and distorted objective realities in the last decade.

Distortion of truth in society

Humans tend to be gullible and deceiving. It has been around since the time of Adam and Eve. God told Adam and Eve not to eat of the fruit from the tree in the middle of the Garden. The serpent, which represented Satan, distorted the truth about God's command by telling Eve that she would be like God if she ate the fruit. Satan, the Father of Lies, wants us to change the definition of truth from objective reality to popular opinion, especially when it tickles our desire for goodness and our drive to excel. Eve desired the knowledge of goodness and to excel like God. So, she ate the forbidden fruit. Once Adam ate

> ### Faith and reason
> ---
> - **Reasoning involves experiences, understanding, judgement, and decision.**
> - **We can choose contrary to reason.**
> - **Reasoning is finite and incomplete.**
> ---
> **We need faith and reason to arrive at the truth.**

the forbidden fruit, he started to point fingers. He distorted the truth by blaming both Eve and God with the statement, "the woman whom you put here with me ...." (Gen 3:12)

One of the common practices to distort the truth is to interpret objective reality of the past with the mentality of the present. For example, today, some people want to tear down statues of George Washington because they viewed him as a racist. Racism is defined as the superiority of one race over another.[57]

Blaming others

The Rebuke of Adam and Eve by Domenichino from Patron's Permanent Fund, Courtesy National Gallery of Art, Washington

Do we distort the truth to put blame on others?

George Washington might have felt superior to the six hundred slaves which he owned, but certainly not to the whole race of Black people. The objective reality of well-to-do families in the 18th century was sadly to own slaves,[58] including African American families.[59] I am not saying that slavery is good. I am saying that we cannot change past objective reality to let our reasoning arrive at a false statement that we call true. Accusing someone falsely as a racist promotes hatred, to the glee of Satan. Another reality is that, in 2021, waiters/waitresses could be paid as low as $2.13 an hour with the understanding they keep all the tips.[60] Such a wage is a far cry from the wage of room and board that the slaves received from George Washington. Besides he, in his will, stated that all slaves were to be freed after the death of his wife.[61]

Another way of distorting the truth is pushing an idea without verifiable facts. In 2019, Nikole Hannah-Jones, published "the 1619 Project," a long-form journalism endeavor, to place "the consequences of slavery and the contributions of Black Americans at the very center of the United States national narrative."[62] She was awarded the 2020 Pulitzer Price for her work. She claimed that the American Revolution was started because the Colonists wanted to protect their right to own slaves. I commend her for an expert journalistic writing in providing a different point of view. However, many states, starting with California, have added Critical Race Theory based on the 1619 Project to their educational curriculum. Distortions to historical truths are being taught to our children. Worse of all, they are being taught to be race-conscious which heightens rather than lessens racial discriminations and tensions. Satan, using opinions, sows seeds of division.

In the last chapter, we said that teaching is a noble profession. Today, teachers have an exceedingly challenging task. They have to (1) decide whether the 1619 curriculum is true or false, (2) if false, withstand popular opinions and/or state mandates not to teach it, and (3) teach their students to become proficient in fact checking from multiple sources especially when media and the "big tech" companies control the distribution of informaton.

For those who have been discriminated and exploited for generations, they demand diversity, equity, and inclusion. Diversity is given. Equity is not the same as equality. If everyone is at the same equity, we have communism. Equality means to treat another equally as oneself and so, we love another as we love ourselves. Inclusion is good but unity is better. Satan uses us to spread negative untruths to promote hatred and disunity. Jesus' last teaching to His disciples, in the form of an intercession, (John 17:19-26) is for love and unity. He prayed that we "may be brought to perfection as one." (John 17:23) Here we learn how to discern about distortions of truth. Do they sow hatred and disunity, or do they sow love and unity? But the cunning serpent will use the words of love and unity to persuade us to adopt the distortions of the truth. The objective reality of our words is verified by their promotion of love and unity.

> ### Distortions of truths in society
>
> ---
>
> - *Interpret past reality with present mentality*
> - *Pushing an ideology without verifiable facts*
>
> ---
>
> ### Consequences:
> - *Defames people's character.*
> - *Alters historical truths.*
> - *Sows hatred, disunity, and societal division.*

Under such distortions of truth by the Father of Lies, we now have people "who call evil good and good evil, who change darkness to light and light to darkness, who change bitter to sweet and sweet to bitter." (Isa 5:20) There is no joy in the mind.

Distortion of truth about self

We also like to deceive ourselves because (1) we do not know who we are, and (2) we want to hide our true personal traits. What defines a person? Before COVID-19 facial coverings, we are recognized by our faces, but they do not define us. In our society, we put a huge emphasis on outward appearances, dietary constraints, organic foods, and physical exercises. We are categorized by where we live, how we dress, the cars we drive, and the restaurants we frequent. But our bodies, habits, and way of life do not define who we are. Nowadays, even our name is no longer unique. My brother had a hard time flying commercially in 2000 when his namesake was on the "no-fly" list. Similarly, educational degrees, ethnicity, and tradition do not define who we are.

Neither do our careers define who we are. At Ford Motor Company I solved problems at the assembly plants because of my understanding of processes and my logical ability to diagnose and resolve issues. I was known as the "go-to" person to resolve plant problems. But neither the title nor my strengths define who I am.

Who am I? Am I defined by

---

my face, body, habits, way of life, name, ethnicity, tradition, education level, or careers?

Rather, I am defined by my behaviors towards God and others in what I think, do, and say, rooted in virtues.

Our behaviors in relation to others, however, do define who we are. Are we kind and considerate, patient, and humble, hardworking, and persistent, etc., or do we exhibit the negative traits like being cruel and self-centered, impatient and proud, lazy and irresolute, etc.? When I talked to other retirees from Ford, we remember our coworkers by their positive or negative character traits. The positive traits come from God who is Love and who is Good. After all, we are His children made in His image. (Gen 1:27) These traits are grounded in virtues. By the grace of God, we can acquire the virtues of prudence, justice, fortitude, and temperance. They are known as the cardinal virtues because all other virtues are grouped around them.

Prudence and temperance help us to respect others regardless of their imperfections. Fortitude and justice bid us to accept others as equal human beings. Fortitude and temperance demand us to be other-centered. Prudence and fortitude beckon us to forgive others. Indeed, all four virtues work together to foster good relationships with others.

It is these same virtues that help us to define our relationship with God. Do we accept God as our creator? Do we have awe and reverence for Him as the all-powerful almighty God? Are we humbled enough to imitate His Love and Goodness to be other-centered? And by the way, God is the other. Are we Christ-centered? His death paid for our sins. Are we willing to offer our being for another to bring others to eternal life?

When we are Christ-centered, do we give priority to Him or to earthly treasures of money, fame, power, sex, food, drink, and other addictions? Jesus teaches that where our treasure is, there our heart will also be. (Matt 6:21) When we pursue secular treasures like science/technology, materialism and possessions, health and external beauty, vain delights and pleasure, or knowledge and power, they become the values of our lives. What are my values? Are they formed around virtues?

Masks and persona

We wear masks to hide our true personal traits. These masks are not the face masks that we wear to protect from the coronavirus. They are persona, which means theatrical mask, e.g., to present ourselves as socially acceptable. They may have severe consequences.

Many people put on the persona that they are happy, but they are not. People like Michael Jackson, Marilyn Monroe, and Robin Williams committed suicides.[63] Instead of hiding a weakness and faking a strength we need to know and be true to ourselves, otherwise we suffer rejection of self. Henri Nouwen says: ""The greatest trap in our life is not success, popularity, or power, but self-rejection."[64]

Wearing masks can begin at a youthful age. In East Asian countries like Japan, Korea and Hong Kong, parents demand exceptional and unreasonable expectations from their children to excel in education. They learn to wear the masks of superiority to avoid peer pressure as well as pressure to excel. In these countries, youth suicides are higher

Persona

Masks by Fritz Baumann from Ailsa Mellon Bruce Fund, Courtesy National Gallery of Art, Washington

Do we mask our shortcomings and try to be someone whom we are not?

than the rest of the world due to the stress to learn and study. In 2015, 70 youths committed suicides in Hong Kong[65] and in February 2017, five youths from secondary schools committed suicides in a 17-day span.[66]

What can I do?

Credit: Rudzhan Nagiev, from istock / Getty Images Plus

**Joy is knowing what we can and cannot do.
And when we do, do the best that we can.**

People with low self-esteem suffer from inferiority complex. In a 2015 survey of 544 teenagers from junior high school to college, 96% responded that they felt inferior at some point in their lives. The top causes of feeling inferior are appearance, ability, and intelligence.[67] For such people, the most common defense mechanisms are the persona of a person who knows everything or can do everything. The sad part is that the poll reports that 82% of the time, people make others feel inferior because they are either inferior or want to feel powerful. Our superiority persona as a result of our own inferiority, not only, hurts ourselves, but others as well.

We also deceive ourselves by wanting a certain career goal which may not be realistic or in tune with our personality. I am too straight forward in my approach to work. I would tell people what was exactly on my mind. Such traits counter those of an executive. Because I am an introvert, I cannot be an effective plant manager either, which job requires finesse. I would have no joy in my life with such careers. From birth, God gave us individual talents to survive as a unique person. This gift of talents allows us to be apostles, teachers, physicians, prophets, etc. (1 Cor 12:28) Some are good in science like the Einstein's of the world. Many excel in music and painting. Some have steady hands and nimble fingers to become skilled surgeons or mechanics. Some are jack of all trades, master in none.

Today, the joy of ownership is not of land, but of "know-how, technology, and skill."[68] Joy in life comes when grace leads us to know our limits and do the best that we can. Indeed, the grace of success lies in knowing what we cannot do. The Serenity Prayer opens with: "God, grant me the serenity to accept things that I cannot change and the courage to change the things that I can."[69] Joy comes from this serenity of knowing our limits and doing the best that we can. There is no joy in the deception of self and one's ability.

Embracing and soaring with one's God-given talents are the key to success according to Steve Harvey, host of the TV show Family Feud and the Miss Universe Pageant.[70] He came from a family with no money, but with faith and work ethics.[71] He had a severe stuttering problem as a child and was teased terribly by classmates at school and in the neighborhood. The counterman at the local deli helped him to overcome the handicap. But the damage was done. Steve could not focus. Though he was the first person in his family to go to college, he flunked out. But he met Arsenio Hall there who impressed him with determination to make it big in Hollywood. After working at various jobs and became separated from his first wife, he spent three years living out of his car. But with determination, he succeeded as a comedian and became renown. He said, "My calling is to help people, to teach people, to share with people, until I die."[72] He lives to make the world a better place.

Distortion of truth about God

Satan wants to separate us from God with lies like God does not exist, He is far away in heaven and does not care about us on Earth, He only loves those upon whom His favor rests, or He creates evil. Mike Lindell lived Satan's lies. He was a crack addict, a card counter gambler, a bar owner, and a drunk. He was arrested, gambled away all his money, and his bar license taken away. For him, God was out of sight and out of mind.

The morning after surrendering his bar to his debtors, Mike was inspired to put on paper the evil of crack. At the end of his writing was the statement, "you will know when the time is right, and you will be given a platform." A few minutes later his sister phoned to say that her pastor said that Mike must follow through on what he wrote.[73] A few months later, he had a dream about pillows. So, he started his pillow company. Amidst his inexperience to manage a company, problems with his cash flow, inventory, marketing, and delivery, and people trying to take over his company, he was still an addict, gambler, and a drunk. But God did not abandon him. He graced Mike with people phoning him so that he can see the truth about himself and the truth about what is good and right. Hence, he had the will to help other addicts to become clean and to set things right with his customers. Then God graced him with practical things, like just in time cash from investors, people to run his company, opportunities to publicize

Distortion of truth about God

God does not exist.

He creates evil.

He does not care about us.

He only loves some of us.

Credit of devil image: Big Bang from Getty istock / Images Plus

from some of Satan's lies.

his company on radio and television, and even a third wife who prays to God. His company became a platform to help other drug addicts. God also graced him to quit as an addict, a gambler, and a drunk.

The mind of Christ

Goodness

He is the Truth which is Goodness and Love. He came to serve with the Truth.

Jesus, the Light of the World, (John 8:12) graced Mike and each of us with the truth about God: His righteousness, (Matt 6:33) His blessings, (Rom 8:32) and His love. (1 John 4:7-16) Because of His righteousness, we know and do, to the best of our abilities, what is good and right. When we see God's blessings in people, nature, and all created things, natural or manufactured, we must give thanks to God in all circumstances. (1Thes 5:18) God loves us beyond our imagination. He is always with us till the end of time (Matt 28:20) Even though we are worthless creatures, having nothing and can do nothing on our own, He promises us to be the vine that supports us. (John 15:5) His great mercy purges our faults and brings our yearnings under control.[74] We must _Forever Rely On God_ (_FROG_) in good or bad times. We rely on Him when we breathe. A friend of mine had a problem with the valve of his heart. He went in for surgery which was totally successful. But his lungs failed to retain oxygen, and he died 3 weeks later.

Joy in the mind

Since our deepest desire is to live forever in the joy of heaven, joy in the mind is to know how to gain eternal life. Jesus teaches, "Now this is eternal life, that they should know you, the only true God, and the one whom you sent, Jesus Christ," (John 17:3) Therefore, to know God the Father and God the Son is to gain eternal life. Only the Son knows the Father (Matt 11:27, John 7:29, 8:55, 10:15, 17:25). So, if we have the mind of Christ, we will know both God the Father and God the Son.

But who can have the mind of Christ? "For my thoughts are not your thoughts, nor are your ways my ways—oracle of the LORD. For as the heavens are higher than the earth, so are my ways higher than your ways, my thoughts higher than your thoughts." (Isa 55:8-9, see also Rom 11:33) Surprisingly, Paul says we have the mind of Christ (1 Cor 2:16) via His Spirit.

After Nebuchadnezzar had exile Jeconiah, king of Judah, to Babylon, Jeremiah said that the Lord will establish a new covenant with remnants of the Israelites: "All, from least to greatest, shall know me, ... for I will forgive their evildoing and remember their sin no more." (Jer 31:34) God wants us back, regardless of our sinfulness, just as He did over and over with the sinful Israelites in the Old Testament. He calls us, His people, as beloved (Rom 9:25). He loves us so much that He calls us His children (Rom 9:26, 2 Cor 6:18) and wants us to dwell with Him so that "there shall be no more death or mourning, wailing or pain." (Rev 21:3-4, see also Ezek 37:27)

Joy in the mind = graced with the truth about God	
Truth about God	**Consequences**
His blessing	Give thanks to Him all the time
His righteousness	Know and do what is good and right
His love	Love and serve others
To know God is eternal life, (John 17:33) our deepest desire.	

He puts a new spirit within us so that we can live by His statutes, careful to observe His decrees. (Ezek 36:27) It is through this gift of the Holy Spirit, which Jesus asked His Father to send to His disciples, (John 14:16-17) that we shall understand the things of God. (1 Cor 2:12) This Spirit of Truth will guide us to all truth, (John 16:13) especially to Christ, who is the Truth. (John 14:6) Since Christ is the Wisdom of God, (1 Cor 1:24), we would have both the Wisdom of God and the Spirit from on high to know God's counsel. (Wis 9:17) And God counsels us to imitate Christ, His Only Son. He came to serve and not to be served. (Mark 10:45) The mind of Jesus, as shown in the Gospels, is to serve others by doing good and loving them. He healed, taught, fed, prayed, offered Himself as our spiritual food and drink, and even died for us.

Joy in our mind, therefore, is to know God: His blessings so that we can thank Him all the time, His righteousness, to do what is right and good, His love, to reflect it by serving and loving others, His encouragement and perseverance, to do the best we can, His care, to know all is well in His Hands, and His faithfulness, to forever rely on Him and trust Him without hesitation. When we know the Truth, Christ Himself, we become holy, fulfilling His prayer to the Father to consecrate us to the truth. (John 17:17) The Truth brings us joy in the mind.

5. Joy in relationship

God created us to be in relationship because He is in relationship![75] The Three Persons in the Trinity exist in relationship. God the Father calls Himself "I am who I am." (Exod 3:14) There can never be an "I" without

The Trinity exists in a relationship.

The Trinity, Anonymous, from Rosenwald Collection, Courtesy of National Gallery of Art, Washington D.C.

It is a communion of Three Persons in love.

a "Thou." Only the divine Son of God can be a "Thou." He is the Word of God. "And the Word was God. He was in the beginning with God. All things came to be through him." (John 1:1-3) Indeed, all things came into being by the word of God as reported in the creation story. (Gen 1:3-27) He is begotten by God the father[76], i.e., generated and not made. He is of the same substance as the Father. Since God is Love, the Son is the mediator who receives and passes on this love[77]. When there is an "I" and a "Thou," there is also a "We." Since, the Holy Spirit is the spiration or the procession from the Father and the Son, He represents the "we." He receives the love and uses it to sanctify humanity for its salvation. Augustine teaches that the Father is the lover, the Son beloved, and the Holy Spirit, the love between them.[78] Augustine defined the Triune relationship as a communion of Three Persons in love.

We begin this chapter with the human desire for relationships. Because it is ingrained in us, it begins at birth. The key to lasting relationships is other-centeredness. Included in it are acceptance and respect, in which communication plays a vital role. Forgiveness is the other aspect of other-centeredness. Because love brings joy, our desire for relationships is a search for love which ends in marriage. We conclude with the unimaginable love that God has for us.

Desire for relationships

When the Son of God became Man, i.e., the Word of God became flesh, (John 1:14) the language of humans became man itself. Therefore, we are born with the desire for relationships. We long to see and talk to people. That is why cell phones and face time are so popular. Martin Cooper, from Motorola, invented "the brick," a handheld cellular mobile phone, which is the size and weight of a brick, in 1973.[79] It replaced the bulky car phones of that era. Twelve years later, a global standard for mobile communication (2G) was developed. Building of digital networks followed. Ten years later, using small lithium-ion batteries, liquid crystal displays, and integrated power radio frequency transistors, mobile phones shrink in size and cost but increase in speed and function. Higher speed networks help to support this growth.[80] By 2013, 40 years after "the brick," almost a billion cell phones were sold.[81]

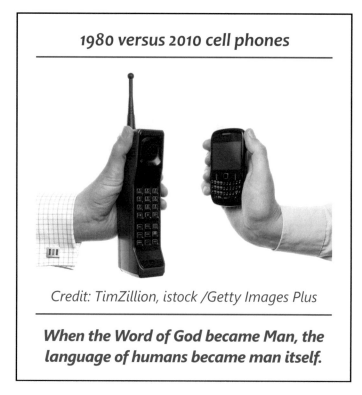

1980 versus 2010 cell phones

Credit: TimZillion, istock /Getty Images Plus

When the Word of God became Man, the language of humans became man itself.

Demand for relationships

By the end of the second trimester a fetus can hear, as evidenced by 24- or 25-week-old premature babies who respond to sounds around them.[82] Therefore, a "fetus can distinguish between the voice of Mom and that of a stranger, and respond to a familiar story read to him/her (it)."[83] How would the baby feel if the mother sings to him/her constantly from nine weeks onwards when the ears are formed? This experience of love from the womb is reinforced at birth when he/she is cuddled and held in his/her mother's arms. It is not a surprise that a new-born infant seeks his/her mother's voice or the rhythm of her heartbeat, which will be replaced later by her touch, smell, warmth, and face.

This demand for relationships is ingrained in us. God realized this when He said: "It is not good for the man to be alone." We, humans, though a lowly creature made by God, are different from all His other creations. God created us to be in communion with others. Hence, He created Eve as "a helper suited for him" (Gen 2:18) to ease Adam's solitude in the Garden of Eden.[84] Aw-zar' is the Hebrew word for help. It is not giving a hand. It means to surround, protect, and aid. It has the sense of "being in it together." We, as a communion of persons, are in it together to have dominion over God's creation (Gen 1:28) to make it better. After Adam's fall, we have the additional goal to return to God's divine life.

Overcoming Adam's solitude,

The Creation of Eve, by Virgil Solis, from Rosenwald Collection, Courtesy of National Gallery of Art, Washington D.C.

God created Eve as a helper or partner for Adam to have dominion over His creation.

This demand for relationships increases with age. My first granddaughter, at four months old, already understood the joy of being in the company of others. She put forth a smile of pure innocent joy when you interacted with her. Her facial demeanor changed immediately when you stopped the interaction and turned away.

My oldest grandson showed, already at 18 months of age, his dissatisfaction with the amount of time that he spent with his parents. His parents interpreted his crying at bedtime as his unwillingness to go to sleep or being afraid of the dark. He, like most children, just wanted to be with his parents as long as he could. He also showed anxiety when his parents or even grandparents would leave him. Children at that age already know who loves them.

At the turn of the century, video games were developed to entertain a team of players. They work together to achieve the common goal in the game. These team games grew in popularity overnight when fueled by the invention of social-media platforms. They echo our natural longing of communion of persons in the sense of "a helper suited for humans." Even in this digital age of cell phones and interactive video games, the punishment that my grandchildren fear most is not being able to go out. It prevents them from mingling and having fun and joy with their friends. They wanted to see each other and talk face to face. "The most terrible poverty is loneliness, and the feeling of being unloved"[85] and unwanted. In 2023, the Surgeon General of the United States issued an advisory on the devasting impact of loneliness.[86] We want companionship. We want to do things together. Instinctively, we see Christ in other people and God's artistry in them.

Joy comes from being with others. It may come in the form of a praise, a kind word, or a generous offer of help. Attention, approval, appreciation, admiration, and affection are some of the free gifts that friends will give to one another and bring joy. We enjoy the goodness of each other, work together, have fun together, and share sadness, happiness, successes, setbacks, likes, dislikes, goals, dreams, a cry, or a laugh. As we share our time, talent, and treasure with others as free gifts, we bring joy to them because we are making the world a better place for them. In return, we experience joy from the good we do and in sharing their joy. Of course, we also receive joy from their gifts of time, talent, and treasure.

Indeed, "life in its true sense is not something we have exclusively in or from ourselves: it is a relationship."[87] To be human is to respond personally in different "I, thou, and we" relationships.[88] We would respond differently to our spouse, children, grandchildren, relatives, friends, teachers, pastor, spiritual director, colleagues, doctors, lawyers, and strangers. And how would we respond to God?

> ### I, Thou, We Relationship
>
> ---
>
> *To be human is to respond personally to different I, thou, we relationships.*
>
> ---
>
> *God is also a Thou. How do we respond to Him?*

Other-centeredness

Because joy comes from being with others, our desire for relationship continues till death. To have a lasting relationship, we need to ask the following: Are my own interests more important than those of others? Am I more important than them? Do I say "yes" to me? Then I am a self-centered person. I only have self-love.

The desire and demand of unconditional love from birth evolves into self-love. It is in the loving of self that the child develops autonomy, initiative, diligence, and identity, thereby accepting his/her own self. Having accepted themselves as who they are, they can then avoid the continual search for perfection and fulfillment of their ego, an unending task with no satisfactory ending. At the same time, they would know their self-limitations and the need for help from others, thereby avoiding falling into the trap of being totally self-centered or selfless to the extreme. Self-love, therefore, is the start of loving one's neighbor.

However, we must teach children to move from self-love back to unconditional love because it is from unconditional love that we learn about mercy, compassion, humility, and service. These are the characteristics of being an authentic human being. Whenever our children experience joy from a gift from another, teach them the link between giving and love.

Jesus, the Good Shepherd, is always other-centered.

Credit: BCWH, istock/ Getty Images Plus

Can we be like Him and be other-centered in our relationships?

Other-centeredness is based on the giving of self. In the giving of self, I learn to be patient rather than angry, listen rather than speak, and say "yes" rather than "no." Jesus was other-centered. He said that the people "were like sheep without a shepherd." (Mark 6:31-34) He forewent time to rest, pray, and eat to minister them. Most of all, He emptied and humbled Himself by becoming human and dying on the cross to pay for our sins (Phil 2:6-8). Can we be like Him and be other-centered in our relationships?

God is also the other. Are we centered on Jesus Christ? Is He number one in our lives? How often do we ask, especially when we are angry or frustrated: "What would You, Jesus, do in this situation?" or "what do You want me to do?" Discerning the will of God is essential so that we are doing His will to be kind and generous. Only then would be Christ-centered. Do we want to have a last relationship with God?

Acceptance and respect

To be other-centered, one must accept and respect another. Acceptance is the acknowledgement that the other person is a human being, equal in every aspect to us, regardless of his/her strengths or weaknesses, status in life, accomplishments or failures, cultural traditions, etc. Often, we respect people for their abilities, qualities and/or achievements, which are natural attractions for us. But respect is the recognition that human beings are beloved children of God. We admire and honor them as our siblings. We afford them the fundamental dignity and rights as children of God. Indeed, as Peter said, "He (God) made no distinction between us and them." (Acts 15:9) Respect does not mean total agreement with the other. Respect challenges assumptions and processes without attacking the person. It enables us to express our concerns with humility and calmness.

Respect and acceptance mean that we must offer help to others because they are human and children of God. For the other person, he/she must also respect and accept the help. When we are down and out, we often pray for miracles like winning the lottery. But most often, God sends us help via another person who may lead us to new opportunities in life. Let us also be open to providing such opportunities to others as God's arms and legs[89] in co-creation.

Acceptance and respect begin with communication. My cousin, Charles Kao, son of my father's sister, was awarded the Nobel Prize in Physics in 2009 for his invention of transmitting light over one hundred kilometers in

Charles Kao awarded 2009 Nobel Prize in Physics.

He invented fiber optics bringing joy through communication, making lives better.

ultra-pure glass fibers. It led to the use of fiber optics for transmission of voice, text, music, and video communications around the world via telephone and broadband internet devices. Today, if we unravel all the fiber optics in a single strand it would be 4.1 billion kilometers long in estimation.[90] My cousin's invention enabled human beings to communicate worldwide literally at the speed of light. His joy is not in the Nobel Prize Award. His joy came from making the lives of human beings better through improved communication. There is no better way to acknowledge another's existence than by communicating with him/her.

Charles spent much of his life trying to connect with others, regardless of whether they are young or old, learned, or uneducated. I remember how he interacted with me over thirty-five years ago when he started the King family reunion. It was a surprise to me that a member of the Kao family would start a reunion for the King's. At the reunion, being 16 years older than me, he talked to me as his equal. He showed sincere interest in me and my work. He listened to me with respect. I remember the joyous twinkle in his eyes and his dignified smile when he connected with me. His behavior overwhelmed me with joy. Though he was not religious, he intuitively knew that God made human beings in His image and likeness (Gen 1:27). Hence, we must dignify and treat each other as equal. To this date, the King Family Reunion, thanks to a member of Kao family, continues annually as the younger generations take over in organizing it.

Communication is not about me. It is about the person with whom I am communicating. What does it take to make that person feel better? How do we lift him/her up with faith, hope, and love? After all we are supposed to make the world a better place one person at a time. "Our savior, Jesus Christ, gave himself for us to … cleanse for himself a people as his own, eager to do what is good." (Tit 2:14)

> ### *God respects and accepts us.*
> ---
> - *He does not interfere with our lives without our permission.*
> - *He accepts us regardless of our sins.*
> - *We are His beloved children.*
> ---
> ***By His grace, we can respect and accept others too!***

With God's grace we change ourselves for the better and be other-centered to accept and respect others as His beloved children. Confucius instructed us by saying that changing the world begins with oneself in a nine-character Chinese phrase: "修身齊家治國平天下." Its meaning is that there is an ordering to bring justice and virtue to the world. The ordering is to cultivate self (修身), manage family (齊家), govern country (治國), then pacify the world (平天下).[91] There is joy in improving oneself as well as changing the world.

Of course, God is also another. Do we accept and respect God? Do we communicate with Him? Prayer is a means of communicating with Him. Do we hear Him? He can talk to us one-to-one, through another person, radio, television, other media, or an event in life. He creates and accepts us first as His beloved children, (Eph 1:5-6) regardless of who we are, what we have done or not done, or whether we thank or trust Him. He respects us so much that He gives us dominion over His creation (Psa 8:6-9) As His children, can we accept Him as our Creator and Father? He loves us beyond our imagination. He even sent His Son to die for us while we are sinners (Rom 5:8) and His Spirit to sanctify us. Can we accept Christ as our Savior, and the Holy Spirit as our Advocate? He respects us so much that He trusts us. Do we respect Him in return? Do we respect Him enough to trust Him in all situations?

Respect is to give special recognition, honor, and high regard. We recognize God as the Almighty Creator by relying on Him with total trust because He knows our desires and fears in our will, joys and heaviness in our hearts, and doubts and certainties in our minds. We honor Him by making Him number one in our lives so that our words and deeds reflect His Love and Goodness. We give Him high regard by thanking Him in all circumstances and praying to Him constantly (1 Thes 5:18) because of His numerous blessings on us.

Joy of forgiveness

Another essential element of other-centeredness is forgiveness. Sin is defined as the breakage of relationships. They can be relationships with us, with God, and/or with others. Some of us are burdened by habitual sin, which I call addiction, e.g., to alcohol, drugs, pornography, video games, work, physical appearance, staying healthy, etc. These sins are mostly against self until the addiction becomes so severe that we cause hurt to someone, e.g.,

> *Joy in relationship*
> *brings joy to heart.*
> _____
> - *Lasting relationships need other-centeredness including*
> - *acceptance and respect,*
> - *and forgiveness*
> _____
> **God wants a lasting relationship with us. Do we have it with Him?**

causing car accidents under the influence of alcohol. There are numerous sins against others. Others include God and people we love most. I tend to get angry with my wife more often than with others. The reason is that she forgives me without waiting for me to ask for forgiveness. Her love triumphs over my sin. Shame on me!

Our sins can be as trivial as being rude or as serious as murder or rape. It can be intentional or spontaneous. These sins, caused by our words and actions, are called sins of commission. We can also sin by our thoughts. How often have we profiled someone in our mind saying that he/she is not competent or not very smart? When I interviewed a candidate for a job, I often made up my mind in the first 60 seconds of the interview whether he/she could do the job. I broke the relationship before it even started.

We can also commit sin against others by our inaction, e.g., when we fail to help someone who is hurt. One of our parishioners, in the middle of February, slipped on ice and fell down the steps in front of the Detroit Court House. He broke his hip and could not get up. Seven people walked by before someone stopped and called an ambulance. These seven strangers committed the sin of omission.

People who commit the sins of omission are often not aware of their failing. We must be extra vigilant and be aware of opportunities to help others, thereby avoiding the sin. Such opportunities provide new adventures and joy to our lives.

Sin causes guilt. Guilt can bring on depression, anxiety disorder, lack of concentration, impaired cognition, and lower productivity. These feelings may also exhibit as physical pains. If the sin is against self, the sinner must forgive himself or herself. If the sin is against another, forgiveness from that person would lift the pain of guilt. Forgiveness brings joy to the sinner.

> *Sin = breakage of relationship*
> ———————————————
> ***Sins of commission and omission bring forth guilt***
> ———————————————
> ***with me, another, and/or God.***

John Paul II was shot by Mehmet Ali Ağca on May 13, 1981.[92] Following the shooting, John Paul II forgave him and asked the world to pray for him. Two years later, John Paul II visited him in prison and verbally delivered his forgiveness. In 2000, the Pope petitioned for his extradition back to Turkey. The Pope practiced what Jesus taught: "Whose sins you forgive are forgiven them, and whose sins you retain are retained." (John 20:23, Matt 18:18) When Jesus addressed this statement to the Apostles, (Matt 16:19) it instituted the Sacrament of Confession. But when He addressed it to the disciples, He addressed it to all Christians. For us, Christians, the statement says that if we do not forgive the sins of our enemies, their sins will be retained. We are personally responsible for the salvation of our enemies. When we fail to forgive their sins, our own sins will not be forgiven either as stated in the Lord's Prayer. (Matt 6:12-15) Indeed, not only are we to forgive, but we are also called to preach forgiveness of sins to all nations (Luke 24:47) telling them that God "will forgive their iniquity and no longer remember their sin." (Jer 31:34)

Hence, the Church offers the Sacrament of Confession for the guilty to ask God for forgiveness. We must repent to receive forgiveness. Christ's death only expiates our sins. Since every sin separates us from God, the Sacrament of Confession is a sacrament of love at which the sinner says sorry to his/her Beloved, God. The priest, *in persona Christi*, lifts the burden of guilt from the sinner, restores his/her relationship with God, gives him hope to lead a life of holiness, and increases his/her faith in the grace of God. The priest, as the representative of the community would often ask the sinner to make amends to those against whom he/she has sinned. Joy comes to those forgiven by God and others.

Relationship of Love

The cry for unconditional love begins in the womb and perpetuates throughout one's life, first as a desire for relationship. As we grow older, this desire becomes one for intimacy to share our lives with another. We move into relationships of love. Love, defined by Pope Benedict XVI, is the "fundamental assent to another, a 'yes' to the person towards whom the love is directed."[93] Just like the love of Christ for us, it is an unconditional, selfless, and limitless acclamation of "yes." It is a "yes" of giving oneself to the beloved. In making such an acclamation of "yes" to us, our lover, selflessly and unconditionally, tries to satisfy our every whim and wish. Therefore, love proceeds from the will,[94] i.e., we choose to love, and to love one person at a time. It is difficult enough to love one person let alone the entire world. There are philanthropists who are working on world problems, like stopping malaria or bringing clean water to those who have none. But these works fulfill their purpose of being co-creators with God. They are not love. Love is free and personal. We give ourselves selflessly, unconditionally, and limitlessly to the beloved.

Joy of Forgiveness – we are responsible for the salvation of our enemies.

Credit: Arturo Mari/Contributor
Getty Images/AFP

"Whose sins you forgive are forgiven them, and whose sins you retain are retained." (John 20:23, Matt 18:18)

My wife gives herself totally to me in this way. She puts up with my idiosyncrasies. She knows me so well that she caters and spoils me. I am all that matters to her. Therefore, her love is liberating for me as she tries to satisfy everyone of my desires. Love, therefore, brings much joy to the heart of the beloved. Because joy is contagious, the lover is also joyful when the beloved enjoys the gifts of love.

In her affirmation of "yes" to me, my wife pronounces that "it is good that I exist"[95] regardless of my imperfections. This affirmation of my existence completes my birth as a human being. I am now a person, a being, for my lover. I can now say "yes" to myself in and together with my lover. I now also live with the satisfaction that there is now a meaning for my existence. I exist for my lover. She needs me as a beloved. Every "mature man (or woman) needs to be needed."[96]

> ## *The beloved becomes the lover.*
> ---
> *The beloved affirms, approves, and accepts the love of the lover, and becomes the lover; and the lover, the beloved.*
> ---
> *Love brings joy to the hearts of both lover and beloved.*

Because this gift of self comes from the heart of the lover, it makes the heart of the beloved flutter with joy. The Chinese defines joy as supreme happiness causing the heart to open or flutter. The Chinese characters for joy are, 開 心. It means literally the opening of the heart. No wonder, my heart flutters when I see my wife. Because love brings joy, we want to be with our lover as often as possible. Hence, the presence of the lover also brings joy to the heart, and we want to live in that presence.

To receive my wife's love, I must affirm, approve, and accept what she does, says, and thinks out of love for me. As part of that affirmation, I would help her in her work. Whether it is housework or yard work, they make me joyful when I realize that I am doing it for her. It is an acclamation of "yes" to her regardless of her imperfections. In that acclamation, I must forgive her and guide her to the truth of her limitations. I tell her that she is wanted, valued, and appreciated. She has become my lover. She, in turn, is being loved and her joy increases. Love, therefore, brings joy to the hearts of both the lover and the beloved.

It is in the law of the gift of self that one learns to reach across the boundary of self and others and allow oneself to be reached. This mutual sharing of one's strength and weaknesses, talents, and deficiencies, hopes and ambitions, joys and sorrows, gains and sacrifices, or work and play enables one to face the challenges of life with others, thereby, increasing the chances of success in overcoming them.

The words: "in giving that we receive"[97] becomes a reality. The Law of the Gift becomes the rule of life because "man finds himself only by making himself a sincere gift to others."[98] John Paul II defines this law as the "law of *ekstasis" or the law of self-giving,*[99] which is the way God lives as described in the next chapter. It is in self-giving that we find fulfillment an*which is the way God lives as described in the next chapter.* It is in self-giving that we find fulfillment and purpose in life and, therefore, happiness. This Law of the Gift, the gift of self totally, unconditionally, selflessly, and limitlessly, is, therefore, the basis of love, and also of joy in the heart.

We recognize that this law of giving myself totally and sincerely to my beloved limits my freedom to do what I want. It is a "yes" that shatters our ego. So, we can only do so with the grace of God. We need the love of Christ, exemplified by the cross, to penetrate us and saturate our ego, so that God can use our heart, mind, will, and body to love another. Only Christ can change our "no" to "yes" as we walk humbly and patiently with Him. And in so doing, I rest in the joy of His love recognizing that He has said "yes" to me over and over in my life.

Our love can be so great that we die for the sake of the beloved because there is no greater love than to lay down one's life for one's friend. (John 15:13) It does not have to be physical death. It is the laying down of our being for our beloved. For example, when the love for one's invalid spouse requires over 30 years of uninterrupted care, it is an absolute gift of oneself.

Marriage – a union of the lover and the beloved

Being loved and being in love are joyful. Marriage is unequivocally one of the fullest joys on earth. It encompasses the joy of giving and receiving each other, of having a new life of sharing with each other in all matters, physical, emotional, and spiritual, and of creating new life. It is the union of a man and a woman as they live with one mind, will, and heart.

The Catholic Church, following Christ's presence at the wedding at Cana, recognizes that marriage is a sacrament, the visible sign of the invisible grace of God. The grace of the presence of Christ in a marriage perfects the couple's love[100] and reduces the burden of marriage.[101] The grace of Christ also strengthens their indissoluble unity.[102] God authors this unity of marriage[103] just as He did when He created Adam and Eve and when He said that the two shall become one. (Gen 2:18-24)

In the wedding ceremony, the wedding couple, who are ministers of the Sacrament of Marriage exchange vows of fidelity and perpetuity of love and honor. They fulfill the vows by their love which is the giving of oneself to the other in mind, heart, will and body. This giving and receiving bring joy to the married couple as they become one in body and soul.

Marriage: one of the fullest joys on earth

Marriage at Cana by Masters of the Catholic Kings, from Samuel H. Kress Collection, Courtesy of National Gallery of Art, Washington D.C.

Christ's presence helps the couple to be one with God and each other.

God loves us beyond our imagination

I would be remiss if I do not say that God is our first lover. (1 John 4:19) He loves us more than we can ever imagine. We received our life, our freedom, and our in-born talents from Him. With our freedom,

He lets us do with what we want with his beautiful creation. He blesses us with our education, careers, successes, family, and possessions. Without Him we can do nothing. (John 15:5) He loves us so much that He wants to spend eternity with us. To do so, He sent His Only Son to be one of us (John 3:16) to suffer and "bore our sins in his body upon the cross" so that by His wounds we are healed allowing us to return to Him, the guardian of our souls. (1 Ptr 2:23-25)

God loves us more than we can ever imagine.

From NASA, Earth Images, https://www.nasa.gov/sites/default/files/thumbnails/image/as17-148-22727_lrg_0.jpg

He loves us first (1 John 4:19) by letting us have dominion over His creation. (Ps 8:6-9) He loves us by wanting to be one with us. (John 17:20-21)

We often miss that God loves us. He gives us the opportunities and the grace to do good deeds which we think that we do on our own. His mercy, not our virtuous deeds, gets us to heaven. We also take for granted our neighbor's acts of love. They are also acts of love from God. Indeed, that is the greatest challenge for us: to know that all good and loving things come from God's mercy. They show the presence of His love. Since His love is the Holy Spirit,[104] God, Himself, is present in our lives here and now. He is always with us, from walks with Adam and Eve (Gen 3:8) till the end of age. (Matt 28:20) Because our deepest desire is to live forever in heaven which means to live in the presence of God, we would also rejoice in His presence here and now with an indescribable and glorious joy. (1 Pt 1:8-9) Jesus affirmed this joy: "I will see you again, and your hearts will rejoice, and no one will take your joy away from you." (John 16:22)

One interpretation of the above statement is that we would be joyful when we go to heaven. Jesus said so Himself: "Now I am coming to you (God the Father). I speak this in the world so that they may share my joy completely." (John 17:13) The other interpretation is that when we live in His presence, i.e., to see Him again here and now, we will be joyful. He promised: "I will not leave you as orphans. I will come to you." (John 14:18) He will reveal Himself to those who love Him. (John 14:21) In fact, He and God the Father will dwell in those who love Him. (John 14:23) The key is to remain in Him, be connected, and be centered on Him all the time whether we are sad or happy, troubled or cared-free, challenged or successful.

God's love for us is so great that He wants more than just being present to us. He wants to be one with us. Jesus said in His prayer at the end of the Last Supper: "I pray ... that they may all be one, as you, Father, are in me and I in you, that they also may be in us." (John 17:20-21) God, by His actions, lives out His covenant to us as in a marriage vow. He has and holds us as His treasures regardless of our situations in life, "for better or worse, richer or poorer, in sickness or in health." He loves and honors us by giving Himself to us totally, unconditionally, and limitlessly via the Holy Spirit. He even sacrificed His Son to die on the cross so that we may be one with Him for all eternity in heaven. No wonder, Paul uses marriage to express the union of Christ with His Church, (Eph 5:21-32) i.e., the people of God. In fact, Jesus calls Himself the bridegroom. (Matt 9:15) Joy in the heart is to be one with God, our lover, and to remain in His love, thereby remaining in Him. Jesus teaches: "If you keep my commandments, you will remain in my love ... I have told you this so that my joy may be in you and your joy may be complete. This is my commandment: love one another as I love you." (John 15:10-12) And so we ask in His name to remain in His love and presence as He said: "In my name, ask and you will receive so that your joy may be complete." (Jn 16:24)

> Joy in the heart is to be with God and remain in His love.

> He lives out His covenant to us as in a marriage vow by giving Himself to us totally, unconditionally, and limitlessly.

> God wants to be one with us. Do we want to be one with Him?

6. Joy in God's Kingdom

God's love for us is unimaginable. He loves us so much that He wants us to be one with Him so that we can experience joy in the mind by knowing Him, joy in the will by doing good as His co-creators, joy in living by fulfilling our desire for goodness, and joy in the heart by remaining in His love. In this chapter we want to show how God blesses us with joy by giving us His Kingdom. And this joy comes from knowing His Goodness and Love, from doing what is good to make the world a better place, and from exercising the law of the gift of self. These attributes are foundational to living in His Kingdom. It is His great gift of freedom that enables us to choose to live in His Kingdom and receive His joy.

God's Kingdom

I am the *Way,*	the way of goodness
the *Truth,*	the truth that God is Good and God is Love
and the *Life*	the life of love

John(14:6)

When our mind knows His Truth, our will does His Way of Goodness, and our life lives His Life of Love, then we live in His Kingdom.

The phrase, Kingdom of God, appears over 130 times in the New Testament. What and where is it? It is where Jesus exercise His dominion. He is the King of kings, Lord of lords. (Rev 19:16, 1 Tim 6:15) He rules over an eternal kingdom as the angel Gabriel told our blessed Mother Mary in the annunciation: "he will rule over the house of Jacob forever, and of his kingdom there will be no end." (Luke 1:32-33) Although physically, we can say that God's Kingdom is the universe and all its living things, but realistically, it is beyond space and time because He is eternal. Our limited intellect cannot grasp God's Kingdom. We only know that we are in it here and now, and God exercises His dominion through us in this time and this space, because we are His arms and legs.[105] Because He gives us the freedom to do what we want with His Kingdom, we receive joy.

Goodness in His Kingdom

Jesus says: "I am the way, and the truth, and the life." (John 14:6) We live in His Kingdom when our mind knows HIs Truth that God is Good, our will does His Way of Goodness, and our heart lives His life of love.

When we exercise our freedom to make God's creation better, we receive countless blessings of good things, from food to shelter, from running water to the internet, from daily conveniences to medical machines, from communication networks to beautiful music, and from cars to movies. And the list is endless. Life in our physical body is a joy because God blesses us with these wonderful basic essential needs which satisfy our desire to survive and with less toil and sweat.

From His grace, His Goodness flows into all the people who serve me directly and indirectly and into all His creations, natural or manufactured. Through them, His numerous blessings overwhelm me.

Thus, I rejoice in His Goodness!

Catherine of Sienna says that

Credit: Orest Lyzhechka from Getty Images Plus / istock

God is "madly" in love with us, lowly creatures. I say He loves us with reckless abandonment. He gave His all to us.

Love in His Kingdom

From the time of creation, we, human beings, have disobeyed God, ignored Him, dumped Him, and even said the He is dead.[106] God be blessed that He did not write us off as a loss. In fact, He wants to be in union with us. He, the Almighty God, became a vulnerable baby in one of the backward Roman territories. This Son of God, Jesus Christ, "gave himself for us to deliver us from all lawlessness and to cleanse for himself a people as his own." (Titus 2:14) His death is the expiation for our sins. His love is so great that even when suffering the most excruciating death on the cross, He asked God the Father to forgive us by crying out: "Forgive them for they know not what they do." (Luke 23:34) He loves us regardless of who we are or what we have done. Because God had become human, He understands that we know not what we do with His great gift of freedom. His Spirit is the breath (ruah), "the force that gives life to all life in the cosmos."[107] He sends His Spirit to reside in us through Baptism. So, He is already in union with us. He just wants us to choose to be in union with Him. Catherine of Sienna said that God is a divine madman; he is drunk with love (ebro d'amore) and he is "mad and wild" with love (pazzo d'amore) for us lowly creatures.[108]

We are God's treasures, loved by Him recklessly.

The Good Shepherd and the lost sheep Credit: duncan1890, DigitalVision Vectors, Getty Image

God loves me individually as if I am the only person in the world.

God is so madly in love with us because we are the crown of His creation. (Psa 8:6) Lawrence, the Archdeacon of Rome under Pope Sixtus II, oversaw the Church's treasury. When asked by the Prefect of Rome to turn over the riches of the Church, Lawrence brought out the lame, the blind, and the indigent declaring that they were the treasures of the Church.[109] Indeed, we are the treasures of God. He rejoices in us like a bridegroom in his bride. (Isa 62:5) His tender and intimate love for us is so great that "He becomes one of us."[110]

I say that God loves us, lowly creatures, extremely with reckless abandonment because He gave His all to us: His creation for us to dominate (Gen 1:28), His Son to die for the expiation of our sins, and His Spirit to unite us with him by enlightening us to the Truth of Christ, encouraging us to live the Way of Christ, and enabling us to imitate the Life of Christ. God is the Law of the Gift of Self.

His unimaginable love is for each of us individually. He loves me as if I am the only person in the world. God exhibits His love, not just by His blessings as discussed in the previous section, but also in His actions to satisfy our deepest desire. He wants us to be in heaven with Him for all eternity. And so, He overlooks my sins for the sake of my repentance. (Wis 11:23) He spares me because He is the lover of all souls, and His imperishable spirit is in me. (Wis 11:26-12:1) He rebukes me little by little and reminds me to abandon my wickedness. (Wis 12:2) The parable of the lost sheep (Matt 18:12, Luke 15:4) tells me that God is reckless enough to leave ninety-nine sheep and search for me when I had wandered off in sin. He never let go. Rather He chases us like the Hound of Heaven.[111] He wants to satisfy our deepest desire to live in joy forever in heaven.

And so, I rejoice in His Love!

Grace in His Kingdom

God is not just an inert entity situated somewhere in heaven. He is continuously active in the life of the universe. For example, His grace enables the Queen of the Night Flower to bloom only for 1 night and perhaps only once in many years.

Our world and the universe continue to evolve. We are His instrument in that evolution, and He continues to run interference in our lives leading us to restore the world. We tend to think of restoration through projects like the green movement.[112] No, God wants to restore us to divine health and to live in divine glory with Him for all eternity in His Kingdom which He has prepared for us

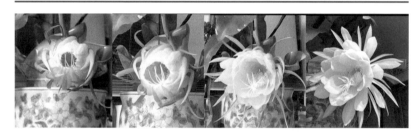

Blooming Sequence of the Queen of the Night

It blooms by God's grace in 1 night and dies in the morning.

We rejoice in the grace of God: His Goodness, His Love, His Righteousness, His Faithfulness, and His Law of Gift.

from the foundation of the world. (Matt 25:34) He sends His Only Son, Jesus Christ, to become human and to die on the cross for the expiation of our sins. Then He raised up Christ from the dead so that we can rise to new life in Christ. He invites us into this new life by self-emptying Himself into us through the Holy Spirit. He calls us in this new life to participate in the flow of His perpetual restoration of humanity and the world. He continues to give all of Himself to us. We are, therefore, recipients of His grace, unmerited divine favor that He pours into our will, mind, and heart. And His grace is abundant and all around us. He just wants us to reach out and grasp it.

We may not know what His grand plan is in this life. We just know that He wants to restore us to divine health. And we are often called to do a small part in His plan because "each one of us is the result of a thought of God. Each one of us is loved, willed, and necessary."[113] God created us, not for naught, but for a definite service to Him, a service uniquely designed for each of us. And He graced us to be His co-workers in this flow of evolution or restoration of His people to divine health. What joy would we get in doing such work!

We must, therefore, listen, trust, and obey His call. Satan deters us from taking these three actions by hitting us with profane feelings of fear, doubt, and pride. Fear of death, risk or uncertainty, and failure are most common. Fear paralyzes us from taking any action after we listen to God. But faith drives away fear. Faith is a theological virtue. It is normally linked to trust in God. The faith that I am talking about is faith in God's creation. He created us in His image. (Gen 1:27) Therefore, He ingrained us with His righteousness. We know what is good and right. Having an action plan to do what is good and right will overcome our fears. Hence, in the listening process, we should listen to both the call to action as well as the plan of action. Then we can discern both the call and the plan for their goodness and righteousness. The grace of righteousness, therefore, moves our will to act after we listen to God's call to restore His people to divine health, i.e., to save their souls.

> ### God graces our
>
> - **will with meaningful and joyful purpose to save souls;**
> - **mind to know that saving souls is good while linking it to the Truth that God is Good and God is Love;**
> - **heart to love Him with total abandonment to Him in the gift of self to save souls.**
>
> **Our joy comes from Christ.**

And so, I rejoice in the grace of righteousness!

God graces our mind to link our knowledge with the Truth that God is Good and God is Love. Because our trust is based on His immense love for us, Satan uses doubt to makes us feel that God does not love us. When blessed with His Goodness and Love, it is easy to trust and offer our happiness, successes, and gratitude to God. But when the storms of life hit us, we must still trust God and offer our challenges: sorrow, sickness, desolation, confusion, frustration, etc., to God because He will use them as He will, including for the salvation of souls. We trust Him because He will not test us beyond our strengths and that He will always help us.

When my job at Ford was eliminated, He found me a new job in less than a week. When I debated a change of career to go work in an assembly plant, He intervened and told me that the work would be beyond my realm of talents. When I was inundated with work, I prayed with three words, "God help me!" I was able to choose what task to discard. This three-word prayer is my favorite one to this day because Jesus says: "ask and you will receive, so that your joy may be complete." (John 16:24)

In fact, He is my rock and my refuge. (2 Sam 22:2, Psa 18:3, 31:3, 62:8, 71:3, 94:22, Isa 17:10) Psalm 91 beautifully describes how God will answer, protect, and deliver those who call Him my refuge and fortress. We must trust this eternal rock (Isa 26:4) in making us worthy of His calling to do Good and to bring to fruition our desire for goodness (2 Thes 1:11) because He will prosper the work of our hands (Psa 90:17) and glorify us in the name of Christ. (2 Thes 1:12) Hence, when we trust in Him, we will be successful in the task of restoring divine health. Jesus reinforces the need to trust in God by saying: ""Let the children come to me; do not prevent them, for the kingdom of God belongs to such as these." (Mark 10:14, Matt 19:14, Luke 18:16) The one common characteristic of all children is their dependency and trust in their parents. We are to trust in and depend on God the Father like little children otherwise we may not enter the Kingdom of God. This grace of trust will move our mind to FROG and to say "yes" to be co-creators with God in restoring divine health.

So, I rejoice in the grace of His Faithfulness and I will *FROG*.

To obey God as His co-creators in restoring divine health and/or making the world a better place for one person at a time, we must ask for the grace to move our heart to serve another. Satan uses pride to make us self-centered rather than Christ-centered and other-centered. Our heart must be moved to accept the grace of obedience from God. I often used the sentence: "When my wife tells me to jump, I jump without even asking how high." Obedience is love. Hence, we surrender ourselves to God. We conform to His will as we pray "let thy will be done" in the Lord's Prayer. Since God the Creator wants us to restore His creation to divine health, we have to offer ourselves to serve others with abandonment just

"Let the children come to me." (Mark 10:4)

Painting in St. Regis Church, Bloomfield Hills, Michigan

Forever rely on God (FROG) the Father like children trusting their parents.

like God's love for us. This is the Law of the Gift. Please note that when we surrender to God's will, we have a firm worthwhile purpose for life. When we do it His way, success is guaranteed. This success helps to make the world a better place, fulfilling our desire for goodness. Hence, we get triple joy.

Christ dies for us to overcome sin and death.

Center Cross at St. Regis Church

So that we can have eternal joy in his presence in heaven.

And so, I rejoice in the grace of His Law of Gift so that I can obey Him and do His will by giving of myself to Him and others.

Expectations

One of the familiar Gospel Readings during the season of Advent (four weeks before Christmas) is the imprisoned John the Baptist. He knew about Jesus' miraculous works. What was his expectation in asking whether Jesus is the Messiah? (Matt 11:2-3) Did he expect Jesus to overthrow the Roman occupation, cast fire down on the Pharisees and Sadducees who were viewed by John the Baptist as a brood of vipers (Matt 3:7), or to get him out of prison like Peter and Paul during their imprisonment (Acts 12:1-19, Acts 16 :16-40)? What do we expect from Jesus?

Before we answer the question, we should ask who is Jesus to us? In the above Gospel reading for Advent, Jesus answered John by saying that the blind sees, deaf hears, mute speaks, lame walks, dead rises, and poor hears the good news. Jesus was quoting from Isaiah. (Isa 35:5-6, 26:19, 61:1) God be blessed that I am not afflicted in the above ways. So, it is hard for me to connect to Jesus through these works of miracles. Intellectually, we all know that Jesus Christ is our God and savior. He, the Son of God, came down from heaven to die on the cross for us to overcome sin and death (1 Cor 15:54-57). At St. Regis, we have a unique cross. The artist portrayed how the death of Jesus changes this world. The wooden cross, representing our world of sin and death, is disintegrating, as Jesus rises in glory towards heaven. Jesus came to heal us spiritually. He wants to restore us to divine health by living according to God's rules and statures. Why? So that we can spend eternity in heaven with Him who loves us more than we can ever imagine. And we have immense joy when we are in the presence of someone who loves us.

Overcoming sin is one way to get back to divine health. We sin when we fail to be a human person and/or when we are self-centered rather than other-centered. For example, I can get drunk and drive recklessly on the expressway causing multiple car crashes and hurting many people. Or I can get angry at my wife. I failed to be human, i.e., I failed to be a child of God. I have become self-centered. Do I expect Jesus to correct my sins? The answer is yes. But Christ may use you to convince me not to get angry or get drunk because you are His arms and legs here on Earth. He may use you as His instrument of my salvation. Indeed, you can expect Christ to use you to overcome the power of sin one person at a time. As a result of your effort, I may not have to suffer everlasting death in the fires of hell.

Inherit the kingdom prepared for you from the foundation of the world. (Matt 25:34)

The Last Judgment from Duomo in Florence. Credit: wjarek, Getty /iStock image plus

Pray for the grace to surrender ourselves to Christ so that we can teach and heal souls.

But still, I must listen to you. And you must be patient because even though Christ is standing at my gates, (Jas 5:7-9) I must open my mind to trust Him and my heart to obey Him. (Jas 4:8) You must be patient until I accept Christ and repent. And you, who are helping me, have moved the head knowledge of Christ being the conqueror of sin and death to heart knowledge. You move towards laying down your life to save my soul. Jesus said: "no one has greater love than this to lay down your life for your friends" (John 15:13) to save their souls. We can expect Christ to use us to save souls.

Happiness, as defined earlier, is contentment with a meaningful purpose. And joy is ultimate happiness. There is no greater meaningful purpose than to save lives. We rejoice when someone's physical life is saved. How much joy would we get when we participate with God to save someone's life for all eternity. This meaningful purpose brings joy to the will because it desires to do good. The mind is joyful when we realize that it is based on the Truth that God is Good and God is Love. And joy in the heart comes from total abandonment to Christ in the giving of self to Christ so that we do what He wants to save souls. Joy is contagious. We bask in the joy of the person whose soul we saved.

How do we save souls here and now? We follow what Jesus did when he was alive on Earth 2000 years ago. He taught and healed others. We expect Christ to guide us and use us to teach others to live in the Kingdom of God, to do what is right in the eyes of God, at the right time for God, and in His way which is the right way. Christ, risen from the dead and ascended into heaven, sends His Spirit into us through the Sacraments of Baptism and Confirmation. Since He is the Power and the Wisdom of God, (1 Cor 1:24) we receive them through the gift of the Holy Spirit. With His Power and Wisdom, we shall have the courage and the know how to proclaim that Christ is "the Lamb of God who takes away the sin of the world." (John 1:29)

> *Least will be greater than John the Baptist (Matt 11:11)*
>
> ---
>
> *if we accept Christ's grace to surrender to Him like a little child to teach and heal so that we can save souls.*
>
> ---
>
> *We proclaim Christ to save souls.*

We can also expect Christ to help us to heal others. There are more people who are spiritually sick than physically sick. They are under Satan's profanities of fear, doubt, and pride. They forget what it means to be human, i.e., to be a child of God. They separate themselves from God the Father, having no dependence on Him and placing self ahead of Him and others. In short, we restore those who do not make God number one in their lives to divine health. In doing so, we reflect His divine glory. To me, God's love is His glory. His love is what makes Him stand head and shoulder above others. Hence, when God gives our heart the grace to love in saving souls by serving others, we live in divine glory again. Can we offer some healing to others, acting as a friend, a family member, a colleague, or a mentor?

We must also expect to help those in physical need by doing works of corporal mercy:[114] feed the hungry, give drink to the thirsty, clothe the naked, shelter the homeless, and visit the sick and imprison. We cannot save their souls unless we help them to stay alive.

Only when we rely on God like a little child would we be able to receive this expected grace from Christ to teach and heal and become His instrument of salvation one person at a time. When we surrender to Him totally then we shall know what to do and say in helping others to come to, to know, and to choose Him. And when we are one in mind, will, and heart with Christ in saving souls, we become the least in the kingdom of God, and yet will be greater than John the Baptist. (Matt 11: 11)

Joy comes from fulfillment of our deepest desire which is to be in heaven for all eternity. We are joyful because in heaven we are in the presence of God who loves us beyond our imagination. He loves us so much that He is "crowning us (me) with love beyond my pow'r to hold."[115] He makes eternity in heaven present to us here and now. Jesus is "Emmanuel, which means God is with us." (Matt 1:23) He promises that He will not leave us as orphans (John 14:18) and that He will be with us always till the end of age. (Matt 28:20)

> **Jesus Christ is the true source of joy**
>
> not because He is the source of our salvation and sanctification but because He loves us beyond our imagination.
>
> Let us live in Him and let Him live in us so that we can experience the joy of His Love and Presence.

When we are one in mind, will, and heart with Christ in saving souls, we live in Him and in His new life, and we let Him live in us. (Gal 1:20) How much more joy can we receive when we live in Christ , and let Him, the true source of joy, live in us?

John teaches that knowing God is eternal life. (John 17:3) But knowing God is not just an intellectual exercise. It is knowing that God gives us the freedom to surrender to Christ and to lead the joyful life of saving souls one person at a time. The joy of eternity is here and now. But we must choose to abide in Christ and let Him live in us. (Gal 1:20) Joy is a choice. Let us pray for the grace to live in Him and serve others through love, (Gal 5:13) thereby bringing them to know and choose God.

Lord Jesus, grant us our deepest desire for eternity in heaven here and now by letting us rest in the joy of your Goodness, Love, and Presence. Grace our mind to know the good you want us to do. Grace our will to realize the good with Your excellence. Grace our heart with Your Love for the person we are serving. It is through your Goodness and Love that he/she would know and choose You. Grace us with Your perseverance and courage in our sacrifice and labor of being Your co-creators. It is in restoring Your creation to divine health that our lives would become meaningful and joyful. Grace us also to live in You by doing your will to save souls with all our will, mind, and heart. And we pray that You live in us so that You are always present to us. We ask all of this in your name, so that we may receive the grace to be your joyful missionary disciples, and our joy will be complete.

Endnotes

1   Aristotle, <u>Nicomachean Ethics</u>, translated by W. D Ross, Book I, Chapter 4, http://classics.mit.edu/Aristotle/nicomachaen.html

2   Roland J. Teske, <u>Henry of Ghent Quodlibetal Questions on Free Will</u>, (Milwaukee: Marquette University Press, 1993), Quodlibetal IX.5, pg. 55

3   Carolyn Gregoire, "Happiness Index: Only 1 In 3 Americans Are Very Happy, According To Harris Poll," The Huffington Post, June 1, 2013, http://www.huffingtonpost.com/2013/06/01/happiness-index-only-1-in_n_3354524.html

4   Pope Paul VI, "Gaudete in Domino, Apostolic Exhortation on Christian Joy," May 9, 1975, #1, http://w2.vatican.va/content/paul-vi/en/apost_exhortations/documents/hf_p-vi_exh_19750509_gaudete-in-domino.html

5   Charles Spurgeon, libquotes.com, To a hungry man, Christ is very lovely when He has a loaf of bread in His hand. (libquotes.com)

6   Nelson, P. & Masel, J. (2017). Intercellular competition and the inevitability of multicellular aging. Proceedings of the National Academy of Sciences, 201618854.

7   Focus Hope, focushope.edu. We note that school-aged children received hot lunches at school.

8   <u>Catechism of the Catholic Church</u>, 2nd edition, Liberia Editrice Vaticana, 1997, #2447

9   Encyclopedia Britannica, Oxygen Cycle, https://www.britannica.com/science/oxygen-cycle

10 Wikipedia, Ecology Geobiochemical Cycles, https://en.wikibooks.org/wiki/Ecology/Biogeochemical_cycles

11 Terry Lindeman, "1.3 Billion Are Living in the Dark," The Washington Post, November 6, 2015, updated November 10, 2015, https://www.washingtonpost.com/graphics/world/world-without-power/

12 Jason Bittel, "60 Percent of the World's Population Still Don't Have the Best Innovation in Human Health" Feb 22, 2013, slate.com, 60 percent of the world population still without toilets. (slate.com)

13 David Blank, "Around 10% of the world population can't get clean water. Here's how you can help on World Water Day," CNN News, March 22, 2020, https://www.cnn.com/2020/03/22/world/world-water-day-03-22-2020-iyw-trnd/index.html

14 Michael H. Crosby, "Thank God Ahead of Time, the Life and Spirituality of Solanus Casey," Franciscan Media, Cincinnati, OH, 2009, p. 76

15 Antislavery.org, "What is modern slavery?" What is modern slavery? - Anti-Slavery International (antislavery.org)

16 St. Augustine, "Confessions," translated by Albert Outler, II.4.9, http://www.ccel.org/ccel/augustine/confessions.iv.html

17 Augustinian Vocations, "St. Augustine and the Pear Tree: A Lasting Story," January 19, 2017, https://augustinianvocations.org/blog-archive/2017/1/19/st-augustine-and-the-pear-tree-a-lasting-story

18 Caroline Castrillon, "Why Chasing Money Alone Won't Make You Happy," Forbes, June 28, 2020, https://www.forbes.com/sites/carolinecastrillon/2020/06/28/why-chasing-money-alone-wont-make-you-happy/?sh=311f8b8d5ded

19 Canadian Poverty Institute, "Poverty in Canada," Poverty in Canada — Canadian Poverty Institute

20 Poverty USA, "The Population of Poverty USA," Poverty Facts (povertyusa.org)

21 Kate Wilkinson, "FACTSHEET: South Africa's official poverty numbers," February 15, 2018, FACTSHEET: South Africa's official poverty numbers - Africa Check

22 Social Metrics Commission, "Measuring Poverty 2020," July 2020, Measuring-Poverty-2020-Web.pdf (socialmetricscommission.org.uk)

23 Arieahn Matamonasa-Bennett, " 'The Poison That Ruined the Nation': Native American Men—Alcohol, Identity, and Traditional Healing," National Center for Biotechnology Information, National Library of Medicine, National Institute of Health, March 26, 2015, "The Poison That Ruined the Nation": Native American Men—Alcohol, Identity, and Traditional Healing - PMC (nih.gov)

24 Aristotle, Nicomachean Ethics, translated by W. D. Ross, I.1, http://classics.mit.edu/Aristotle/nicomachaen.html

25 Vatican Council II Documents, Pastoral Constitution on the Church in the Modern World, Gaudium et spes, ed. Austin Flannery, (Northport, NY: Costello Publishing, 1996), #16

26 Francis de Sales, "Introduction to the Devout Life," Christian Classics Ethereal Library, Grand Rapids, MI, Introduction to the Devout Life (ccel.org), Part I, Ch 1, pg. 10

27 Statistics about Infertility, http://www.wrongdiagnosis.com/i/infertility/stats.htm

28 Infertility, Facts, Prevention, and Treatment Strategies, http://www.healingwithnutrition.com/idisease/infertility/infertility.html#A1

29 Wikipedia, "Maslow's hierarchy of needs," Maslow's hierarchy of needs - Wikipedia

30 F K Beller, G P Zlatnik, "The beginning of human life," National Center for Biotechnical Information, National Library of Medicine, National Institute of Health, September 12, 1995, https://pubmed.ncbi.nlm.nih.gov/8589565/#:~:text=Embryonic%20and%20fetal%20life%20are,the%20beginning%20of%20human%20life

31 The Guardian, "Lost on the Front Line," archived on Oct 27, 2021, Lost on the frontline: US healthcare workers who died fighting Covid-19 | US news | The Guardian

32 Center for Disease Control and Prevention, "Motor Vehicle Crash Deaths," last updated July 6, 2016. https://www.cdc.gov/vitalsigns/motor-vehicle-safety/index.html#infographics

33 Council of Economic Advisors, The White House, "State of Homelessness in America," September 2019, https://www.whitehouse.gov/wp-content/uploads/2019/09/The-State-of-Homelessness-in-America.pdf

34 Food Research and Action Center, "Hunger and Poverty in America," https://frac.org/hunger-poverty-america

35 Psychology Today, "Happiness," https://www.psychologytoday.com/intl/basics/happiness

36 Blaise Pascal, "Pensées," translated by Jonathan Bennett, 2017, https://www.earlymoderntexts.com/assets/pdfs/pascal1660.pdf

37 Pope Leo XIII, "Encyclical Rerum Novarum, on Capital and labor," May 15, 1891, #44, https://www.vatican.va/content/leo-xiii/en/encyclicals/documents/hf_l-xiii_enc_15051891_rerum-novarum.html

38 US Government Accounting Office, "Millions of People May Still be Eligible for Covid-19 Stimulus Payments, But Time is Running Out," October 11, 2022, https://www.gao.gov/blog/millions-people-may-still-be-eligible-covid-19-stimulus-payments-time-running-out

39 Hayden Dublois and Jonathan Ingram, "How the New Era of Expanded Welfare Programs is Keeping Americans from Working," September 11, 2021, Foundation for Government Accountability, https://www.google.com/search?q=what+is+fga.org&oq=what+is+fga.org&aqs=chrome..69i57j0i13i512l4j0i10i13i512l3j0i13i512l2.17959j1j7&sourceid=chrome&ie=UTF-8

40 Pope John Paul II, "Encyclical Letter Centesimus Annus, on the Hundredth Anniversary of Rerum Novarum," May 1, 1991, #31, https://www.vatican.va/content/john-paul-ii/en/encyclicals/documents/hf_jp-ii_enc_01051991_centesimus-annus.html

41 Ibid, #32

42 Thérèse of Lisieux, Story of a Soul, translated by Ronald Knox, (NY, Kennedy & Sons, 1958), p. 236

43 Pope John Paul II, "Fides et Ratio, encyclical letter on the relationship between faith and reason," September 14, 1998, #28, http://www.vatican.va/content/john-paul-ii/en/encyclicals/documents/hf_jp-ii_enc_14091998_fides-et-ratio.html

44 Augustine, "Confessions," translated and edited by Albert C. Outler, Book X, Chapter 23, #33, http://www.fordham.edu/halsall/basis/confessions-bod.html

45 Pope John Paul II, Fides et Ratio, #28

46 Jay Richardson, "Cherry Tree Myth," National Library for the Study of George Washington, Cherry Tree Myth · George Washington's Mount Vernon

47 Pope Benedict XVI, "The Yes of Jesus Christ," Crossroad Publishing Company, New York, NY, 1991, pp. 86-87

48 Microsoft Bing, "Covid Trends," death in the US from covid 19 - Bing

49 Encyclopedia Britannica, "History of Empiricism," empiricism - History of empiricism | Britannica

50 Frederick Copleston, A History of Philosophy, Vol. 4, (NY: Image Books, 1994), 91.

51 Jamie Frater, "Top 10 Incorrupt Corpses," August 21, 2007, Listverse, Top 10 Incorrupt Corpses - Listverse

52 The Catholic Church declared someone as a saint when 2 proven miracles occurred after people prayed to that person after his/her death. Usually, these miracles are miracles of healing. In 2019, 5 new saints were named. See Katherine Ruddy, "Meet the five new saints of the Catholic Church," October 14, 2019, Aleteia, 5 new saints of the Catholic Church (aleteia.org)

53 Steven Hawking, Gödel and the End of Physics, lecture at the University of Texas, A&M, March 8, 2003, http://www.physics.sfasu.edu/astro/news/20030308news/StephenHawking20030308.htm

54 John Paul II, Fides et Ratio, opening paragraph, p.7

55 Jean Paul Sartre, No Exit, http://en.wikipedia.org/wiki/No_Exit

56 Stanford Encyclopedia of Philosophy, Friedrich Nietzsche, http://plato.stanford.edu/entries/nietzsche/

57 Dictionary.com, "Racism," Racism | Definition of Racism at Dictionary.com

58 Ann Brown, "Fact Check: What Percentage of White Southerners Owned Slaves?" the Moguldom Nation, August 10, 2020, Fact Check: What Percentage Of White Southerners Owned Slaves? (moguldom.com)

59 Harry Noyes, "How many black slave-owners were there prior to the American Civil War?" quora.com, August 6, 2018, (3) How many black slave-owners were there prior to the American Civil War? - Quora

60 U.S. Department of Labor, "Minimum Wages for Tipped Employees," January 1, 2021, Minimum Wages for Tipped Employees | U.S. Department of Labor (dol.gov)

61 Wikipedia, "List of presidents of the United States who owned slaves," https://en.wikipedia.org/wiki/List_of_presidents_of_the_United_States_who_owned_slaves

62 Wikipedia, "The 1619 Project," The 1619 Project - Wikipedia

63 Aiden Mason, "20 Famous Actors Who Committed Suicide," TV Over Mind, 2018, https://www.tvovermind.com/actors-who-committed-suicide/

64 Inspiringquotes.us, "Henri Nouwen Quotes and Sayings," Top 30 quotes of HENRI NOUWEN famous quotes and sayings | inspringquotes.us (inspiringquotes.us)

65 Wikipedia, "2015-2017 Youth Suicides in Hong Kong," https://en.wikipedia.org/wiki/2015–2017_youth_suicides_in_Hong_Kong

66 Cherie Chan, "Why are Hong Students Committing Suicide?" Deutsche Welle Broadcasting, April 13, 2017, https://www.dw.com/en/why-are-hong-kong-students-committing-suicide/a-38414311

67 "Teen Poll on Self Worth," Stages of Life, February 2015, https://www.stageoflife.com/Portals/0/High%20School%20Images/WritingContest/Polls/2015-Feb/Teen-Statistic-Self-Worth.pdf

68 Pope John Paul II, Centesimus Annus, #32

69 Praywithme.com, "The Serenity Prayer," The Serenity Prayer - "God Grant Me The Serenity to Accept..." (praywithme.com)

70 Kirsten Acuna, "The one thing every successful person needs to do, according to Steve Harvey," Business Insider, January 26, 2016, https://www.businessinsider.com/steve-harvey-every-successful-person-has-to-jump-2016-1

71 Leah Rosen, "Steve Harvey on Success and His Hard-Won Life Lessons: "I'm Living Proof You Can Reinvent Yourself," Parade Entertainment, October 3, 2014, https://parade.com/340210/leahrozen/steve-harvey-on-success-and-his-hard-won-life-lessons-im-living-proof-you-can-reinvent-yourself/

72 Ibid.

73 Mike Lindell, "What are the Odds? From Crack Addict to CEO," 2019, Lindell Publishing, Chaska, MN, pp. 119-120

74 Bernard of Clairvaux, "Sermon 74 on the Song of Songs," in Louis Dupré and James A. Wiseman, p. 111

75 Josie Siler, "What Did Jesus Mean When He Said 'I and the Father Are One'?" Crosswalk.com, 'I and the Father Are One' - Meaning of Jesus' Words in Bible Verse (crosswalk.com)

76 The Nicean Creed, https://www.usccb.org/beliefs-and-teachings/what-we-believe

77 Walter Kasper, The God of Jesus Christ, translated by Matthew J. O'Connell, (New York, Crossroads, 1977), p. 308.

78 Augustine, On the Trinity, XV, 17, https://www.newadvent.org/fathers/130115.htm

79 Catie Watson, "Facts About How The First Cell Phone Was Invented," Techwalla, Aug 29, 2019, https://www.techwalla.com/articles/facts-about-how-the-first-cell-phone-was-invented

80 Wikipedia, "Mobile Phone," https://en.wikipedia.org/wiki/Mobile_phone

81 Eric Zeman, "1 Billion Smartphones Shipped In 2013," January 8, 2014, 1 Billion Smartphones Shipped In 2013 (informationweek.com)

82 Janet L. Hopson, Fetal Psychology, Psychology Today, Vol 31, Issue 5, Sept/Oct 1998, pp 44-49, http://www.leaderu.com/orgs/tul/psychtoday9809.html

83 Ibid.

84 John Paul II, "The Meaning of Man's Original Solitude," General Audience, Wednesday 10 October 1979, https://www.vatican.va/content/john-paul-ii/en/audiences/1979/documents/hf_jp-ii_aud_19791010.html

85 Mother Teresa, from Good Reads, https://www.goodreads.com/quotes/50997-the-most-terrible-poverty-is-loneliness-and-the-feeling-of

86 Vivek H. Murthy, "Our Epidemic of Loneliness and Isolation," Surgeon General Advisory, US Department of Health and Human Services, May 3, 2023, https://www.hhs.gov/sites/default/files/surgeon-general-social-connection-advisory.pdf

87 Pope Benedict XVI, "Spe Salvi, Encyclical Letter on Christian Hope," November 30, 2007, #27, http://www.vatican.va/holy_father/benedict_xvi/encyclicals/documents/hf_ben-xvi_enc_20071130_spe-salvi_en.html

88 Walter Kasper, <u>The God of Jesus Christ</u>, translated by Matthew J. O'Connell, (New York: Crossroads, 1997), 290

89 Overall Motivation, "65 St. Teresa of Avila Quotes on Success in Life," 65 Saint Teresa of Avila Quotes On Success In Life – OverallMotivation

90 Fiber Optic Social Network, May 4, 2022, https://www.fomsn.com/forum/topic/how-many-kilometers-of-optical-fiber-cables-have-been-laid-worldwide-as-of-the-year-2017/?amp

91 The quote that appears in Remez Sasson, "60 Confucius Quotes and Sayings," https://www.successconsciousness.com/blog/quotes/confucius-quotes/ is "To put the world right in order, we must first put the nation in order; to put the nation in order, we must first put the family in order; to put the family in order, we must first cultivate our personal life; we must first set our hearts right." It is a very long translation of Confucius' nine-character phrase.

92 Wikipedia, "Mehmet Ali Ağca," https://en.wikipedia.org/wiki/Mehmet_Ali_A%C4%9Fca

93 Pope Benedict XVI, "The Yes of Jesus Christ," p. 89

94 Thomas Aquinas, I.93.6, http://newadvent.org/summa/1093.htm#article6

95 Ibid.

96 Erik Erikson, <u>Childhood and Society</u>, Second Edition, (Norton, 1963), p. 266. Parenthetical remark added by author.

97 Prayer of St. Francis, https://www.catholicnewsagency.com/resource/55030/peace-prayer-of-st-francis-of-assisi

98 <u>Pastoral Constitution on the Church in the Modern World, Gaudium et spes</u>, #24

99 Edward Sri, "The Law of the Gift: Understanding the Two Sides of Love," Catholic Education Resource Center, September/October 2005, https://www.catholiceducation.org/en/controversy/marriage/the-law-of-the-gift-understanding-the-two-sides-of-love.html

100 <u>Catechism of the Catholic Church</u>, #1651

101 Ibid., #1615

102 Ibid., #1614

103 Ibid., #1603

104 St. Augustine, "On the Trinity," Book VIII, chapter 10, Christian Classics Ethereal Library, https://archive.org/stream/OnHolyTrinityAugustine/On%20Holy%20Trinity%20Augustine_djvu.txt

105 Overall Motivation, "65 St. Teresa of Avila Quotes on Success in Life."

106 Wikipedia, "God is Dead," God is dead - Wikipedia

107 Richard Rohr, "Daily Meditation: The Spirit is a Life Force," Center for Action and Contemplation, June 8, 2022, Richard Rohr Daily Meditation: The Spirit Is a Life-Force | Cac.org (newslettercollector.com)

108 Peter Rosengren: "A God so in love with us … He becomes one of us," December 25, 2018, Australian Catholic Weekly, A God so in love with us … He becomes one of us | The Catholic Weekly

109 Wikipedia, "Saint Lawrence," Saint Lawrence - Wikipedia

110 Rosengren

111 Francis Thompson, "The Hound of Heaven," http://www.houndofheaven.com/poem

112 "Green Movement," Encyclopedia.com, May 14, 2018, https://www.encyclopedia.com/history/modern-europe/russian-soviet-and-cis-history/green-movement

113 Pope Benedict XVI, Homily at the Mass of the Imposition of the Pallium and Conferral of the Fisherman's Ring, April 24, 2005, 24 April 2005: Mass for the inauguration of the Pontificate | BENEDICT XVI (vatican.va)

114 Catechism of the Catholic Church, #2447

115 Marty Haugen, "Psalm 23." GIA Publications, Inc., Chicago, IL, 1986

Printed in the United States
by Baker & Taylor Publisher Services